NEW AND REVISED EDITION

Golf Rules in Pictures

Illustrated by George Kraynak

AN OFFICIAL PUBLICATION OF
The United States Golf Association®

A GD/PERIGEE BOOK

Perigee Books
are published by
The Putnam Publishing Group
200 Madison Avenue
New York, New York 10016

Writing and interpreting the Rules of Golf are just two of the services of the
United States Golf Association. The USGA also conducts 12 national championships, provides national handicapping and course rating systems, maintains golf's
most complete museum and library collection, and conducts turfgrass research
and course maintenance programs. The USGA performs these and other services
for the good of the game.
    For information on how you can support the USGA, call: 1-800-223-0041

SUPPORT THE USGA ASSOCIATES PROGRAM

Library of Congress Cataloging in Publication Data

United States Golf Association.
    Golf rules in pictures.

"An official publication of the United States Golf Association."
Includes complete text of the Rules of golf as approved by the United States Golf Association and
the Royal and Ancient Golf Club of St. Andrews.
1. Golf—Rules. I. Kraynak, George. II. Royal and Ancient Golf Club of St. Andrews. III. United
States Golf Association. Rules of golf. 1984. IV. Title.
    GV971.U5   1984   796.352'02'022   83-26345
            ISBN 0-399-50984-4

First GD/Perigee printing, 1984

Printed in the United States of America
Fourth Impression

Contents

Introduction

The Rules of Golf were first codified little more than two hundred years ago by one organization—the Honourable Company of Edinburgh Golfers, in Edinburgh, Scotland. That initial code, written in 1744, consisted of thirteen regulations, beginning with the instruction that "the ball must be teed within two club-lengths of the hole." How was the ball teed? On a little mound of soil. And where did the soil come from? Inside the hole, of course. When play of the hole was completed, the player merely scooped a little dirt from inside the hole, built a small mound and then set his ball upon it. So much for uniform-sized holes. The regulation that set the diameter of the hole at four and one-quarter inches and its depth at least four inches came much later.

The fact that the ball was teed within two club-lengths of the hole also meant that putting greens of two centuries ago were less than the impeccably groomed surfaces we see in our United States Open Championship of today. As conditions became more favorable for putting, inventive souls created new instruments to help them. One, for instance, attached a spirit level to his putter, but that was in violation of a Rule that had been developed much later than those original thirteen regulations and designed to maintain the game in its traditional form.

Today the Rules are written by two organizations—the United States Golf Association and the Royal and Ancient Golf Club of St. Andrews, Scotland. These Rules are in effect wherever golf is played, whether it be a weekend four-ball at your Club or for many thousands of dollars on the professional tour. Representatives from both the USGA and the R&A meet regularly every four years to confer on the Rules and to make adjustments and to clarify them where it is deemed necessary, for golf is a dynamic game and the Rules must stay apace of new developments. Golf is played, also, over a vast expanse—indeed at least 125 acres is needed for a standard eighteen-hole course—and the opportunity for original and unusual situations is limitless. The two organizations met most recently in May 1983, and effected the first comprehensive revision of the Rules of Golf since 1952. In revising the Rules, the USGA and the R&A attempted, where feasible, to simplify them as well. These Rules went into effect on January 1, 1984.

The object of this book is to make some of the fundamental Rules situations come to life. The bare bones of the code are presented in drawings.

As you read *Golf Rules in Pictures,* note that the Rules present many rights for the player. It is not a code of purely restrictive covenants; rather it is an expression of all the golfing customs that generations of sportsmen have found fairest for all. The Rules are just a reflection of the sporting ways of playing the game. They therefore carry privileges as well as obligations.

In examining any picture and the relative text, the reader will find it worthwhile to refer to the complete Rule on the subject at the back of the book.

The illustrative material in this book was compiled by Joseph C. Dey, the former Executive Director of the United States Golf Association, C. Edmund Miller, the former Executive Assistant, and by myself.

P. J. BOATWRIGHT, JR.
Executive Director, Rules and Competitions,
United States Golf Association

Etiquette

CONSIDERATION FOR OTHER PLAYERS

No one should move, talk or stand close to or directly behind the ball or the hole when a player is addressing the ball or making a stroke.

DON'T DELAY

Players should play without delay.

SAFETY FIRST

No player should play until the players in front are out of range.

SEARCHING FOR BALL—PLAYING THROUGH

Players searching for a ball should allow other players coming up to pass them; they should signal to the players following them to pass, and should not continue their play until those players have passed and are out of range.

PRIORITY ON THE COURSE

If a match fails to keep its place on the course and loses more than one clear hole on the players in front, it should allow the match following to pass.

HOLES IN BUNKERS

Before leaving a bunker, a player should carefully fill up and smooth over all holes and footprints made by him.

RESTORE DIVOTS, REPAIR BALL-MARKS AND DAMAGE BY SPIKES

Through the green, a player should ensure that any turf cut or displaced is replaced at once and pressed down and that any damage to the putting green made by the ball is carefully repaired. Damage to the putting green caused by golf shoe spikes should be repaired *on completion of the hole.*

DAMAGE TO GREENS

RIGHT

WRONG

Players should ensure that, when putting down bags or the flagstick, no damage is done to the putting green and that neither they nor their caddies damage the hole by standing close to it, in handling the flagstick or in removing the ball from the hole. The flagstick should be properly replaced in the hole before the players leave the putting green. Players should not damage the putting green by leaning on their putters, particularly when removing the ball from the hole.

Definitions

ADDRESSING THE BALL

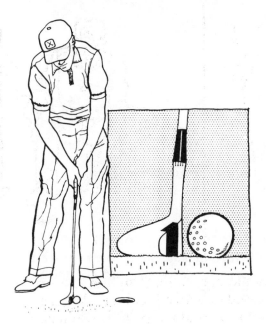
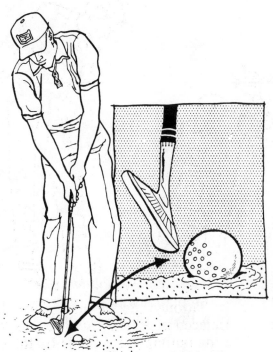

A player has "addressed the ball" when he has taken his *stance* and has *also* grounded his club, except that in a *hazard* a player has addressed the ball when he has taken his stance.

ADVICE

"Is my grip right?"

"Is the penalty one or two strokes?"

"Advice" is any counsel or suggestion which could influence a player in determining his play, the choice of a club, or the method of making a stroke.

Information on the Rules or on matters of public information, such as the position of hazards or the flagstick on the putting green, is not advice.

BUNKER

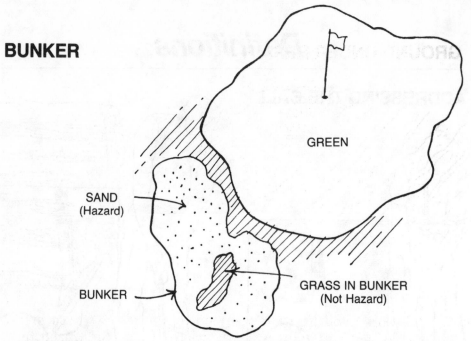

A "bunker" is a *hazard* consisting of a prepared area of ground, often a hollow, from which turf or soil has been removed and replaced with sand or the like. Grass-covered ground bordering or within a bunker is not part of the bunker.

CASUAL WATER

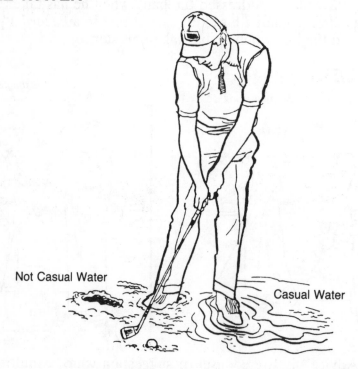

"Casual water" is any temporary accumulation of water on the *course* which is visible before or after the player takes his *stance* and is not in a *water hazard*. Snow and ice are either casual water or *loose impediments,* at the option of the player. Dew is not casual water.

12

GROUND UNDER REPAIR

"Ground under repair" is any portion of the *course* so marked by order of the Committee or so declared by its authorized representative. It includes material piled for removal and a hole made by a greenkeeper, even if not so marked. Stakes and lines defining ground under repair are in such ground.

Note 1: Grass cuttings and other material left on the course which have been abandoned and are not intended to be removed are not ground under repair unless so marked.

Note 2: The Committee may make a Local Rule prohibiting play from ground under repair.

LOOSE IMPEDIMENTS

"Loose impediments" are natural objects such as stones, leaves, twigs, branches and the like, dung, worms and insects and casts or heaps made by them, provided they are not fixed or growing, are not solidly embedded and do not adhere to the ball.

Sand and loose soil are loose impediments on the *putting green*, but not elsewhere.

Snow and ice are either *casual water* or loose impediments, at the option of the player.

Dew is not a loose impediment.

LOST BALL

"I've found your first ball!"

"I can't play that one— this one's in play now."

"Here's your original ball."

"Too late. I've just played the provisional from here."

A ball is lost if:

a. It is not found or identified as his by the player within five minutes after the player's side or his or their caddies have begun to search for it; or

b. The player has put another ball into play under the Rules, even though he may not have searched for the original ball; or

c. The player has played any stroke with a *provisional ball* from the place where the original ball is likely to be or from a point nearer the hole than that place, whereupon the provisional ball becomes the *ball in play*.

Time spent in playing a *wrong ball* is not counted in the five-minute period allowed for search.

14

BALL DEEMED TO MOVE

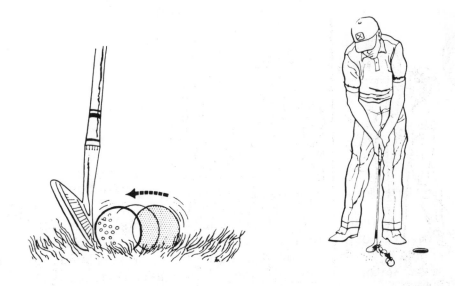

A ball is deemed to have "moved" if it leaves its position and comes to rest in any other place.

OBSTRUCTIONS

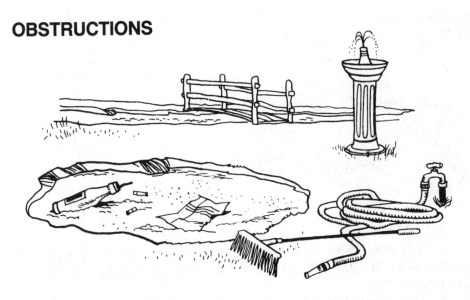

An "obstruction" is anything artificial, including the artificial surfaces and sides of roads and paths, except:

a. Objects defining *out of bounds*, such as walls, fences, stakes and railings;

b. Any part of an immovable artificial object which is out of bounds; and

c. Any construction declared by the Committee to be an integral part of the course.

OUT OF BOUNDS

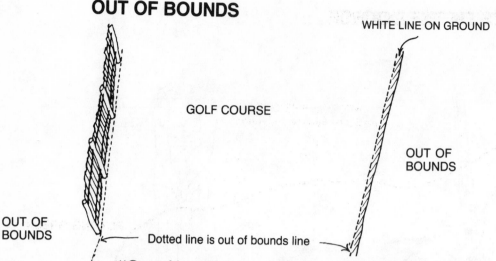

WHITE LINE ON GROUND

GOLF COURSE

OUT OF BOUNDS

OUT OF BOUNDS

Dotted line is out of bounds line

"Out of bounds" is ground on which play is prohibited.

When out of bounds is defined by reference to stakes or a fence or as being beyond stakes or a fence, the out of bounds line is determined by the nearest inside points of the stakes or fence posts at ground level excluding angled supports.

When out of bounds is defined by a line on the ground, the line itself is out of bounds.

The out of bounds line is deemed to extend vertically upward and downward.

A ball is out of bounds when all of it lies out of bounds.

A player may stand out of bounds to play a ball lying within bounds.

OUTSIDE AGENCY— RUB OF THE GREEN

An "outside agency" is any agency not part of the match or, in stroke play, not part of a competitor's side, and includes a referee, a marker, an observer or a forecaddie. Neither wind nor water is an outside agency.

A "rub of the green" occurs when a ball in motion is accidentally deflected or stopped by an *outside agency* (see Rule 19–1).

PARTS OF THE COURSE

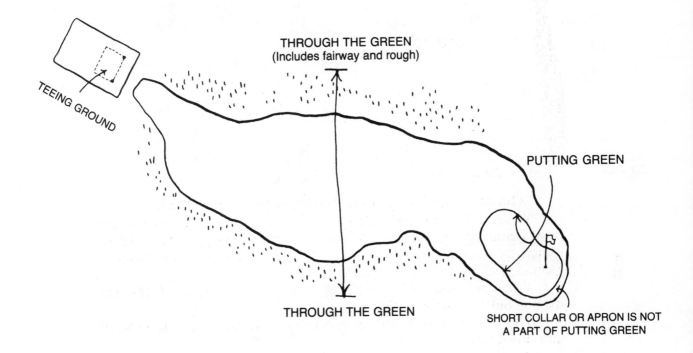

Putting Green

The "putting green" is all ground of the hole being played which is specially prepared for putting or otherwise defined as such by the Committee.

A ball is on the putting green when any part of it touches the putting green.

Teeing Ground

The "teeing ground" is the starting place for the hole to be played. It is a rectangular area two club-lengths in depth, the front and the sides of which are defined by the outside limits of two tee-markers. A ball is outside the teeing ground when all of it lies outside the teeing ground.

Through the Green

"Through the green" is the whole area of the course except:
a. The *teeing ground* and *putting green* of the hole being played;
b. All *hazards* on the course.

SIDES AND MATCHES

Threesome

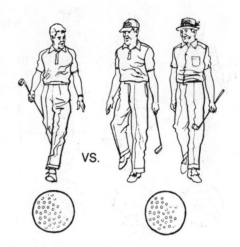

A threesome is a match in which one plays against two, and each side plays one ball.

Foursome

A foursome is a match in which two play against two, and each side plays one ball.

Three-Ball

A three-ball is a match in which three play against one another, each playing his own ball.

A best-ball is a match in which one plays against the better ball of two or the best ball of three players.

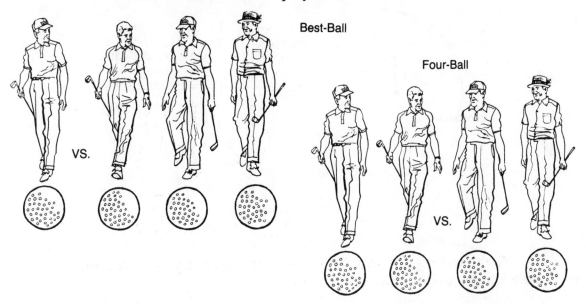

Best-Ball

Four-Ball

A four-ball is a match in which two play their better ball against the better ball of two other players.

STROKE

A "stroke" is the forward movement of the club made with the intention of fairly striking at and moving the ball.

WATER HAZARDS AND LATERAL WATER HAZARDS

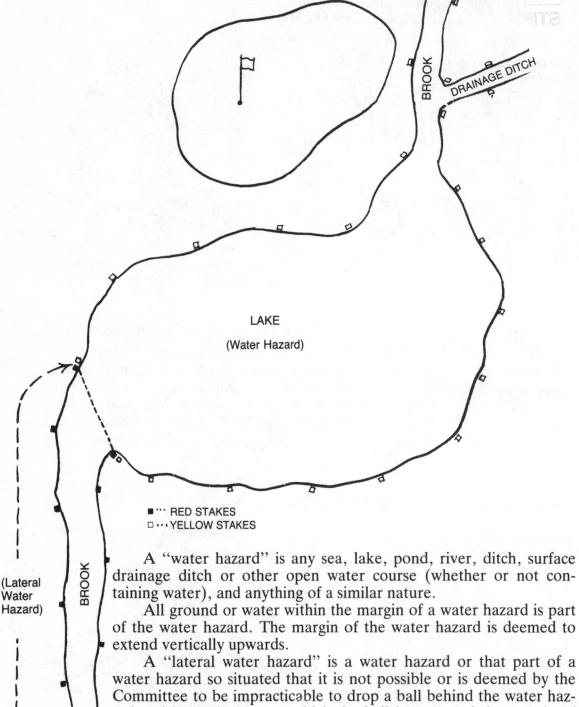

LAKE

(Water Hazard)

■ ··· RED STAKES
□ ··· YELLOW STAKES

(Lateral Water Hazard)

BROOK

BROOK

DRAINAGE DITCH

A "water hazard" is any sea, lake, pond, river, ditch, surface drainage ditch or other open water course (whether or not containing water), and anything of a similar nature.

All ground or water within the margin of a water hazard is part of the water hazard. The margin of the water hazard is deemed to extend vertically upwards.

A "lateral water hazard" is a water hazard or that part of a water hazard so situated that it is not possible or is deemed by the Committee to be impracticable to drop a ball behind the water hazard and keep the spot at which the ball last crossed the margin of the hazard between the player and the hole.

That part of a water hazard to be played as a lateral water hazard should be distinctively marked. Stakes and lines defining the margins of hazards are in the hazards.

Note: water hazards should be defined by yellow stakes or lines and lateral water hazards by red stakes or lines.

The Rules of Play

STIPULATED ROUND; THE GAME

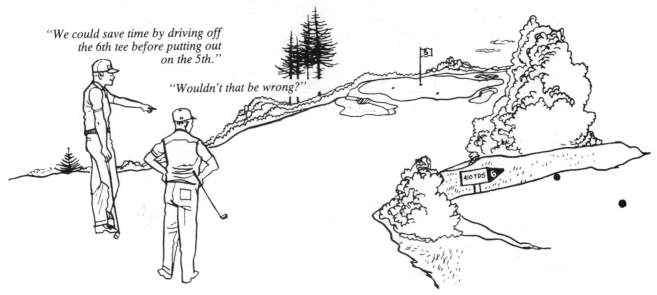

"We could save time by driving off the 6th tee before putting out on the 5th."

"Wouldn't that be wrong?"

The "stipulated round" consists of playing the holes of the course in their correct sequence unless otherwise authorized by the Committee. The number of holes in a stipulated round is eighteen unless a smaller number is authorized by the Committee.

The Game of Golf consists in playing a ball from the *teeing ground* into the hole by a *stroke* or successive strokes in accordance with the Rules. PENALTY: *Match play—Loss of hole; Stroke play—Disqualification.* **Rule 1–1.**

AGREEMENT TO WAIVE RULES

"Shall we play distance only for out of bounds?"

"No, indeed. We'll play by the Rules of Golf."

Players shall not agree to exclude the operation of any Rule or to waive any penalty incurred. PENALTY: *Match play—Disqualification of both sides; Stroke play—Disqualification of competitors concerned.* **Rule 1–3.**

MATCH PLAY

DETERMINING A WINNER

9-Hole Match

HOLE	1	2	3	4	5	6	7	8	9	OUT
FRANK	5	5	3	3	4	4	4			
BOBBY	4	4	2	3	4	4	4			

Bobby winner
of match
3 up and 2
to play

Holes Won — Holes Halved

Winner of Hole

In match play the game is played by holes.

Except as otherwise provided for in the Rules, a hole is won by the side that holes its ball in the fewer strokes. In a handicap match the lower net score wins the hole. **Rule 2–1.**

AN AUTOMATIC HALF

Mr. B is preparing to play his 4th stroke.

Mr. A, who has holed out in 4, says to Mr. B, "Your putt is going to break to the left."

Halved Hole

A hole is halved if each side holes out in the same number of strokes.

When a player has holed out and his opponent has been left with a stroke for the half, if the player thereafter incurs a penalty, the hole is halved. **Rule 2–2.**

Reckoning of Holes

The reckoning of holes is kept by the terms: so many "holes up" or "all square," and so many "to play."

A side is "dormie" when it is as many holes up as there are holes remaining to be played. **Rule 2–3.**

Winner of Match

A match (which consists of a *stipulated round,* unless otherwise decreed by the Committee) is won by the side which is leading by a number of holes greater than the number of holes remaining to be played.

A side may concede a match at any time prior to the conclusion of the match.

The Committee may, for the purpose of settling a tie, extend the stipulated round to as many holes as are required for a match to be won. **Rule 2–4.**

CLAIMS IN MATCH PLAY

"Did you break a Rule on the last hole when you dropped away from that fence?"

Claims

In match play, if a doubt or dispute arises between the players and no duly authorized representative of the Committee is available within a reasonable time, the players shall continue the match without delay. Any claim, if it is to be considered by the Committee, must be made before any player in the match plays from the next teeing ground or, in the case of the last hole of the match, before all players in the match leave the putting green.

No later claim shall be considered unless it is based on facts previously unknown to the player making the claim and the player making the claim had been given wrong information (Rules 6–2a and 9) by an opponent. In any case, no later claim shall be considered after the result of the match has been officially announced, unless the Committee is satisfied that the opponent knew he was giving wrong information. **Rule 2–5.**

STROKE PLAY

DETERMINING A WINNER

HOLE	OUT	10	11	12	13	14	15	16	17	18	IN	TOTAL
FRANK	38	5	3	3	4	5	4	3	4	5	36	74
BOBBY	35	5	4	4	4	5	5	3	4	3	37	72

Bobby is the winner

The competitor who plays the *stipulated round* or rounds in the fewest strokes is the winner. **Rule 3–1.**

FAILURE TO HOLE OUT

"This is a gimme."

"No! This is stroke play. You must hole out."

If a competitor fails to hole out at any hole before he has played a *stroke* from the next *teeing ground,* or, in the case of the last hole of the round, before he has left the *putting green, he shall be disqualified.* **Rule 3–2.**

DOUBT AS TO PROCEDURE

In stroke play only, when during play of a hole a competitor is doubtful of his rights or procedure, he may, without penalty, play a second ball. After the doubtful situation has arisen and before taking further action, he should announce to his marker his decision to proceed under this Rule and which ball he will score with if the Rules permit.

On completing the round, the competitor must report the facts immediately to the Committee; if he fails to do so, *he shall be disqualified.* If the Rules allow the procedure selected in advance by the competitor, the score with the ball selected shall be his score for the hole. If the competitor fails to announce in advance his procedure or selection, the ball with the higher score shall count if the Rules allow the procedure adopted for such ball. **Rule 3–3.**

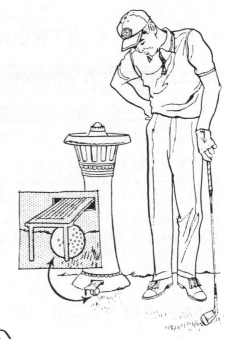

GENERAL PENALTY

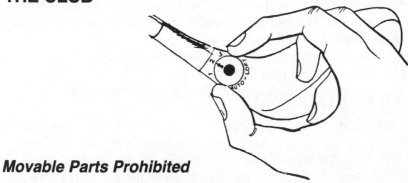

"There's no penalty given for breaking that Local Rule."

Except when otherwise provided for, the PENALTY for a breach of a Rule is: *Match play—Loss of hole; Stroke play—Two strokes.* **Rule 2–6 and 3–5.**

THE CLUB

Movable Parts Prohibited

The club shall be composed of a shaft and a head. All parts of the club shall be fixed so that the club is one unit. The club shall not be designed to be adjustable except for weight. The club shall not be substantially different from the traditional and customary form and make. **Rule 4–1a.**

THE GRIP

CLUB GRIP CIRCULAR

PUTTER GRIP FLAT SIDE (Permitted on Putters only)

The grip consists of that part of the shaft designed to be held by the player and any material added to it for the purpose of obtaining a firm hold. The grip shall be substantially straight and plain in form and shall not be molded for any part of the hands. Except for putters, the grip must be generally circular in cross-section. A putter grip may have a non-circular cross-section, provided the cross-section has no concavity. **Rule 4–1c and App. II.**

MAXIMUM OF FOURTEEN CLUBS

"Let's be sure I have only fourteen clubs."

Selection and Replacement of Clubs

The player shall start a *stipulated round* with not more than fourteen clubs. He is limited to the clubs thus selected for that round except that, without unduly delaying play, he may:

(i) if he started with fewer than fourteen, add as many as will bring his total to that number; and

(ii) replace, with any club, a club which becomes unfit for play in the normal course of play.

The addition or replacement of a club or clubs may not be made by borrowing from any other person playing on the course. PENALTY: *Match play—At the conclusion of the hole at which the breach is discovered, the state of the match shall be adjusted by deducting one hole for each hole at which a breach occurred. Maximum deduction per round: two holes. Stroke play—Two strokes for each hole at which any breach occurred; maximum penalty per round: four strokes.* **Rule 4–4a.**

Excess Club Declared Out of Play

Any club carried or used in breach of this Rule shall be declared out of play by the player immediately upon discovery that a breach has occurred and thereafter shall not be used by the player during the round. PENALTY: *Disqualification*. **Rule 4–4c.**

THE BALL

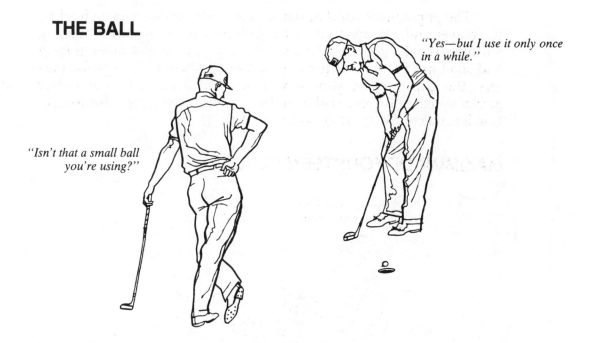

"Isn't that a small ball you're using?"

"Yes—but I use it only once in a while."

The weight of the ball shall *not* be *greater* than 1.620 ounces avoirdupois, and the size *not less* than 1.680 inches in diameter.
PENALTY: *Disqualification*. **Appendix III a and b.**

BALL UNFIT FOR PLAY

A ball is unfit for play if it is visibly cut or out of shape or so cracked, pierced or otherwise damaged as to interfere with its true flight or true roll or its normal behavior when struck. A ball is not unfit for play solely because mud or other materials adhere to it, its surface is scratched or its paint is damaged or discolored.

If a player has reason to believe his ball has become unfit for play during play of the hole being played, he may during the play of such hole lift his ball without penalty to determine whether it is unfit, provided he announces his intention in advance to his opponent in match play or his marker or a fellow-competitor in stroke play and gives his opponent, marker or fellow-competitor an opportunity to examine the ball. If he lifts the ball without announcing his intention in advance or giving his opponent, marker or fellow-competitor an opportunity to examine the ball, *he shall incur a PENALTY of one stroke.* **Rule 5–3.**

"I'm going to play this cut ball on this water hole."

"Then you can't change the ball on the green."

If it is determined that the ball has become unfit for play during play of the hole being played, the player may substitute another ball, placing it on the spot where the original ball lay. Otherwise, the original ball shall be replaced.

If a ball breaks into pieces as a result of a stroke, the stroke shall be replayed without penalty (see Rule 20–5). *PENALTY for breach of Rule 5–3: *Match play—Loss of hole; Stroke play—Two strokes.*

*If a player incurs the general penalty for breach of Rule 5–3, no additional penalty under the Rule shall be applied.

Note 1: The ball may not be cleaned to determine whether it is unfit for play—See Rule 21.

Note 2: If the opponent, marker or fellow-competitor wishes to dispute a claim of unfitness, he must do so before the player plays another ball.

PLAYER'S RESPONSIBILITIES

CONDITIONS OF COMPETITION

The player is responsible for knowing the conditions under which the competition is to be played. **Rule 6–1.**

CHECKING HANDICAP

Match Play

Before starting a match in a handicap competition, the player shall declare to his opponent the handicap to which he is entitled under the conditions of the competition. If a player declares and begins the match with a higher handicap, which would affect the number of strokes given or received, *he shall be disqualified;* otherwise, the player shall play off the declared handicap. **Rule 6–2a.**

Stroke Play

In any round of a handicap competition, the competitor shall ensure that the handicap to which he is entitled under the conditions of the competition is recorded on his score card before it is returned to the Committee. If no handicap is recorded on his score card before it is returned, or if the recorded handicap is higher than that to which he is entitled and this affects the number of strokes received, *he shall be disqualified* from that round of the handicap competition; otherwise, the score shall stand. **Rule 6–2b.**

Note: It is the player's responsibility to know the holes at which handicap strokes are to be given or received.

BREACH OF RULE BY CADDIE

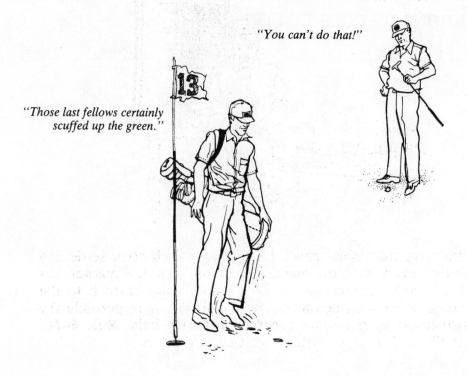

"You can't do that!"

"Those last fellows certainly scuffed up the green."

For any breach of a Rule by his caddie, the player incurs the relative penalty. **Rule 6–4.**

IDENTIFICATION MARK ON BALL

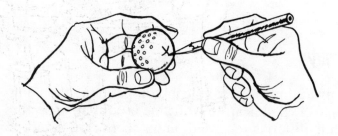

The responsibility for playing the proper ball rests with the player. Each player should put an identification mark on his ball. **Rule 6–5.**

CHECKING SCORES
IN STROKE PLAY

The competitor shall check his score for each hole, settle any doubtful points with the Committee, ensure that the marker has signed the card, countersign the card himself and return it to the Committee as soon as possible. The competitor is responsible for the correctness of the score recorded for each hole. **Rule 6–6b.** PENALTY for breach of Rule 6–6b: *Disqualification.*

NO ALTERATION OF SCORES IN STROKE PLAY

"May I see that card I turned in about an hour ago? I think I put down a 5 for the 18th, but I actually had a 6."

No alteration may be made on a card after the competitor has returned it to the Committee.

If the competitor returns a score for any hole lower than actually taken, *he shall be disqualified.* If he returns a score for any hole higher than actually taken, the score as returned shall stand. **Rule 6–6c.**

Note: In four-ball stroke play, see also Rule 31–4 and 31–7a.

UNDUE DELAY

The player shall play without undue delay. Between completion of a hole and playing from the next tee, the player shall not unduly delay play. **Rule 6–7.** PENALTY for breach of Rule: *Match play— Loss of hole; Stroke play—Two strokes. For repeated offense—Disqualification.*

If the player delays play between holes, he is delaying the play of the next hole, and the penalty applies to that hole.

DISCONTINUANCE OF PLAY

The player shall not discontinue play unless:
(i) the Committee has suspended play;
(ii) he believes there is danger from lightning;
(iii) he is seeking a decision from the Committee on a doubtful or disputed point (see Rules 2–5 and 34–3); or
(iv) there is some other good reason such as sudden illness.
Bad weather is not of itself a good reason for discontinuing play.

If the player discontinues play without specific permission from the Committee, he shall report to the Committee as soon as practicable. If he does so and the Committee considers his reason satisfactory, the player incurs no penalty. Otherwise, *the player shall be disqualified.* **Rule 6–8a.**

Exception in match play: Players discontinuing match play by agreement are not subject to disqualification unless by so doing the competition is delayed.

Note: Leaving the course does not of itself constitute discontinuance of play.

PRACTICE

BEFORE OR BETWEEN ROUNDS

1st hole

Match Play

On any day of a match play competition, a player may practice on the competition *course* before a round. **Rule 7–1a.**

Stroke Play

On any day of a stroke competition or play-off, a competitor shall not practice on the competition *course* or test the surface of any putting green on the course before a round or play-off. When two or more rounds of a stroke competition are to be played over consecutive days, practice between those rounds on any competition course remaining to be played is prohibited. PENALTY: *Disqualification.* **Rule 7–1b.**

Exception: Practice putting or chipping on or near the first *teeing ground* before starting a round or play-off is permitted.

DURING ROUND

"Watch out, Hank; I'm playing another shot for practice."

During Play of Hole

"As long as we have to wait, don't you think it would be all right if we tried a few practice putts on the 9th green?"

Between Holes

"Can't do it—it's against the Rules."

A player shall not play a practice *stroke* either during the play of a hole or between the play of two holes except that, between the play of two holes, the player may practice putting or chipping on or near the *putting green* of the hole last played, any practice putting green or the *teeing ground* of the next hole to be played in the round, provided such practice stroke is not played from a hazard and does not unduly delay play. **Rule 7–2.** PENALTY for breach of Rule 7-2: *Match play—Loss of hole; Stroke play—Two strokes.*

In the event of a breach between the play of two holes, the penalty applies to the next hole.

Note: A practice swing is not a practice *stroke* and may be taken at any place, provided the player does not breach the Rules.

ADVICE; INDICATING LINE OF PLAY

GIVING OR ASKING FOR ADVICE

"Fine shot.
What club did you use?"

Except as provided in Rule 8–2, a player may give advice to, or ask for advice from, only his partner or either of their caddies. **Rule 8–1.**

INDICATING LINE OF PLAY

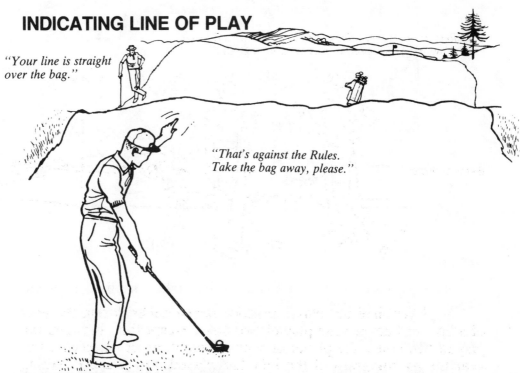

"Your line is straight over the bag."

"That's against the Rules. Take the bag away, please."

Other Than on Putting Green

Except on the *putting green,* a player may have the line of play indicated to him by anyone, but no one shall stand on or close to the line while the *stroke* is being played. Any mark placed during the play of a hole by the player or with his knowledge to indicate the line shall be removed before the stroke is played. **Rule 8–2a.**

Exception: Flagstick attended or held up—Rule 17–1.

On the Putting Green

When the player's ball is on the *putting green,* the player's caddie, his partner or his partner's caddie may, before the *stroke* is played, point out a line for putting, but in so doing the putting green shall not be touched in front of, to the side of, or behind the hole. No mark shall be placed anywhere on the putting green to indicate a line for putting. **Rule 8–2b.** PENALTY for breach of Rule: *Match play—Loss of hole; Stroke play—Two strokes.*

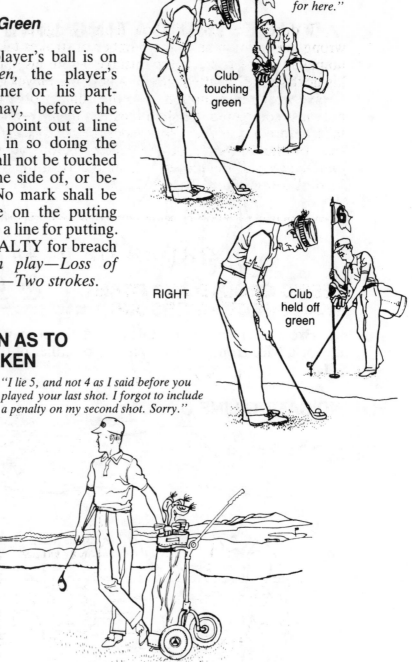

WRONG

"Putt it for here."

Club touching green

RIGHT

Club held off green

INFORMATION AS TO STROKES TAKEN

"I lie 5, and not 4 as I said before you played your last shot. I forgot to include a penalty on my second shot. Sorry."

General

The number of strokes a player has taken shall include any penalty strokes incurred. **Rule 9–1.**

Match Play

A player who has incurred a penalty shall inform his opponent as soon as practicable. If he fails to do so, he shall be deemed to have given wrong information, even though he was not aware that he had incurred a penalty.

An opponent is entitled to ascertain from the player, during the play of a hole, the number of strokes he has taken and, after play of a hole, the number of strokes taken on the hole just completed.

If during the play of a hole the player gives or is deemed to give wrong information as to the number of strokes taken, he shall incur no penalty if he corrects the mistake before his opponent has played his next stroke. If after play of a hole the player gives or is deemed to give wrong information as to the number of strokes taken on the hole just completed, he shall incur no penalty if he corrects his mistake before any player plays from the next *teeing ground* or, in the case of the last hole of the match, before all players leave the *putting green*. If the player fails so to correct the wrong information, *he shall lose the hole*. **Rule 9–2.**

ORDER OF PLAY

TEEING GROUND AND OTHER THAN ON TEEING GROUND

Match Play and Stroke Play

On the teeing ground, the side with the honor shall play first. Other than on the teeing ground, the ball farther from the hole shall be played first. If two balls are equidistant from the hole, the ball to be played first should be decided by lot. **Rules 10–1a and 1b and 10–2a and 2b.**

Exceptions: Rule 30–3c (best-ball and four-ball match play).
Rule 22 (ball interfering with or assisting play).
Rule 31–5 (four-ball stroke play).

PLAYING OUT OF TURN

"I believe it was my honor."

Match Play

If a player plays when his opponent should have played, the opponent may immediately require the player to abandon the ball so played and, without penalty, play a ball in correct order. **Rule 10–1c.**

Stroke Play

If a competitor plays out of turn, no penalty shall be incurred and the ball shall be played as it lies. If, however, the Committee determines that competitors have agreed to play in an order other than that set forth in Clauses 2a and 2b of this Rule to give one of them an advantage, *they shall be disqualified.* **Rule 10–2c.**

SECOND BALL FROM TEEING GROUND

Who drives next?

Out of Bounds

If a player plays a *provisional ball* or a second ball from a *teeing ground,* he should do so after his opponent or fellow-competitor has played his first *stroke.* If a player plays a provisional ball or a second ball out of turn, Clauses 1c and 2c of this Rule shall apply. **Rule 10–3.**

TEEING GROUND

BALL FALLING OFF TEE

If a ball, when not *in play,* falls off a tee or is knocked off a tee by the player in addressing it, it may be re-teed without penalty, but if a *stroke* is made at the ball in these circumstances, whether the ball is moving or not, the stroke shall be counted but no penalty shall be incurred. **Rule 11–2.**

PLAYING OUTSIDE TEEING GROUND

Stance legal   Ball's position wrong

Match Play

If a player, when starting a hole, plays a ball from outside the *teeing ground,* the opponent may immediately require him to replay stroke from within the teeing ground, without penalty. **Rule 11–3a.**

Stroke Play

If a competitor, when starting a hole, plays from outside the *teeing ground, he shall be penalized two strokes* and shall then play a ball from within the teeing ground. Strokes played by a competitor from outside the teeing ground do not count in his score. If the competitor fails to rectify his mistake before making a *stroke* on the next teeing ground or, if the last hole of the round, before leaving the *putting green, he shall be disqualified.* **Rule 11–3b.**

Teeing

A player may stand outside the *teeing ground* to play a ball within it. When the first *stroke* with any ball (including a *provisional ball*) is played from the teeing ground, the tee-markers are immovable *obstructions* (see Rule 24–2). **Rule 11–1.**

SEARCHING FOR BALL;
IDENTIFYING BALL

SEEING BALL

Are you always allowed to see the ball when you play?

A player is not necessarily entitled to see the ball when playing a stroke. If a ball lies in long grass, rushes, bushes, whins, heather or the like, only so much thereof may be touched as will enable the player to find and identify his ball, except that nothing shall be done which improves its lie, the area of his intended swing or his line of play. **Rule 12–1.**

SEARCHING FOR BALL

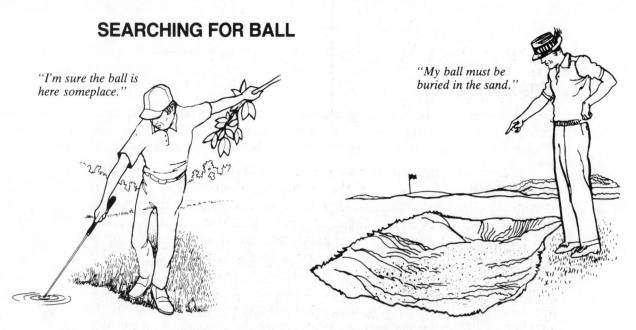

"I'm sure the ball is here someplace."

"My ball must be buried in the sand."

In a *hazard,* if the ball is covered by *loose impediments* or sand, the player may remove only as much thereof as will enable him to see a part of the ball. If the ball is moved in such removal, no penalty is incurred and the ball shall be replaced. As to removal of loose impediments outside a hazard, see Rule 23.

If a ball lying in *casual water, ground under repair* or a hole, cast or runway made by a burrowing animal, a reptile or a bird is accidentally moved during search, no penalty is incurred; the ball shall be replaced, unless the player elects to proceed under Rule 25–1b.

If a ball is believed to be lying in water in a *water hazard,* the player may probe for it with a club or otherwise. If the ball is moved in so doing, no penalty shall be incurred; the ball shall be replaced, unless the player elects to proceed under Rule 26–1. (Continuation of **Rule 12–1**). PENALTY for breach of Rule 12–1: *Match play— Loss of hole; Stroke play—Two strokes.*

IDENTIFYING BALL

May he lift the ball?

Yes   No   Sand in bunker

Except in a *hazard,* the player may, without penalty, lift a ball he believes to be his own for the purpose of identification and clean it to the extent necessary for identification. If the ball is the player's ball, he shall replace it on the spot from which it was lifted. Before the player lifts the ball, he shall announce his intention to his opponent in match play or his marker or a fellow-competitor in stroke play and give his opponent, marker or fellow-competitor an opportunity to observe the lifting and replacement. If he lifts the ball without announcing his intention in advance or giving his opponent, marker or fellow-competitor an opportunity to observe, or if he lifts his ball for identification in a hazard, *he shall incur a penalty of one stroke* and the ball shall be replaced. **Rule 12–2.**

BALL PLAYED AS IT LIES; AREA OF INTENDED SWING AND LINE OF PLAY; STANCE

BALL PLAYED AS IT LIES

The ball shall be played as it lies except as otherwise provided in the Rules. **Rule 13–1.** (Ball at rest moved, see Rule 18.)

IMPROVING LIE, AREA OF INTENDED SWING OR LINE OF PLAY

Except as provided in the Rules, a player shall not improve or allow to be improved:

the position or lie of his ball,

the area of his intended swing or

his line of play

by any of the following actions:

moving, bending or breaking anything growing or fixed (including objects defining *out of bounds*) or

removing or pressing down sand, loose soil, replaced divots, other cut turf placed in position or other irregularities of surface except as follows:

as may occur in fairly taking his *stance,*

in making a *stroke* or the backward movement of his club for a stroke,

on the *teeing ground* in creating or eliminating irregularities of surface, or

on the *putting green* in removing sand and loose soil as provided in Rule 16–1a or in repairing damage as provided in Rule 16–1c.

"Do you want me to hold back this limb?"

How hard may the player press down the grass?

The club may be grounded only lightly and shall not be pressed on the ground. **Rule 13–2.**

Exception: Ball lying in or touching hazard (Rule 13–4).

BUILDING STANCE

This is wrong

A player is entitled to place his feet firmly in taking his stance, but he shall not build a stance. **Rule 13–3.**

BALL LYING IN OR TOUCHING HAZARD

Touching hazard is not allowed

Water

Bunker

Loose impediments must not be touched

Except as provided in the Rules, before making a *stroke* at a ball which lies in or touches a *hazard* (whether a *bunker* or a *water hazard*), the player shall not:

a. Test the condition of the hazard or any similar hazard,

b. Touch the ground in the hazard or water in the water hazard with a club or otherwise, or

c. Touch or move a *loose impediment* lying in or touching the hazard.

Exceptions:

1. At address or in the backward movement for the stroke, the club may touch any obstruction or any grass, bush, tree or other growing thing.

2. The player may place his clubs in a *hazard,* provided nothing is done which may constitute testing the soil or improving the lie of the ball.

3. The player after playing the stroke, or his *caddie* at any time without the authority of the player, may smooth sand or soil in the hazard, provided that, if the ball still lies in the hazard, nothing is done which improves the lie of the ball or assists the player in his subsequent play of the hole. **Rule 13–4**. PENALTY for breach of Rule: *Match play—Loss of hole; Stroke play—Two strokes.*

Smoothing Irregularities

Bunker

STRIKING THE BALL

BALL TO BE FAIRLY STRUCK AT

WRONG

The ball shall be fairly struck at with the head of a club and must not be pushed, scraped or spooned. **Rule 14–1.**

ASSISTANCE

In making a stroke a player shall not accept physical assistance or protection from the elements. **Rule 14–2.** PENALTY for breach of Rule 14–1 or –2: *Match play—Loss of hole; Stroke play—Two strokes.*

ARTIFICIAL DEVICES AND UNUSUAL EQUIPMENT

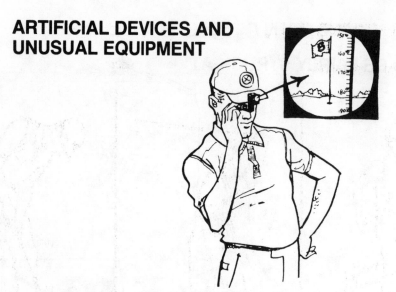

Except as provided in the Rules, during a stipulated round the player shall not use any artificial device or unusual equipment:

a. For the purpose of gauging or measuring distance or conditions which might affect his play; or

b. which might assist him in gripping the club, in making a stroke or in his play, except that plain gloves may be worn, resin, tape or gauze may be applied to the grip (provided such application does not render the grip nonconforming under Rule 4–1c), and a towel or handkerchief may be wrapped around the grip. **Rule 14–3.** PENALTY for breach of Rule 14–3: *Disqualification*.

STRIKING BALL MORE THAN ONCE

If a player's club strikes the ball more than once in the course of a *stroke,* the player shall count the stroke and *add a penalty stroke,* making two strokes in all. **Rule 14–4.**

PLAYING MOVING BALL

Playing a moving ball is prohibited . . .   . . . but . . .

IN WATER HAZARD

A player shall not play while his ball is moving. **Rule 14–5.**
Exceptions:
Ball falling off tee—**Rule 11–2.**
Striking the ball more than once—**Rule 14–4.**
Ball moving in water—**Rule 14–6.**
When the ball begins to move only after the player has begun the *stroke* or the backward movement of his club for the stroke, he shall incur no penalty under this Rule for playing a moving ball, but he is not exempt from any penalty incurred under the following Rules:
Ball at rest moved by player—**Rule 18–2a.**
Ball at rest moving after address—**Rule 18–2b.**
Ball at rest moving after loose impediment touched—**Rule 18–2c.**

Ball Moving in Water

When a ball is moving in water in a *water hazard,* the player may, without penalty, make a *stroke,* but he must not delay making his stroke in order to allow the wind or current to improve the position of the ball. A ball moving in water in a water hazard may be lifted if the player elects to invoke Rule 26. **Rule 14–6.** PENALTY for breach of Rule 14–5 or –6: *Match play—Loss of hole; Stroke play—Two strokes.*

PLAYING A WRONG BALL

General

A player must hole out with the ball played from the *teeing ground* unless a Rule permits him to substitute another ball. **Rule 15–1.**

Match Play

If a player plays a stroke with a *wrong ball*, except in a *hazard, he shall lose the hole.* When the player and the opponent exchange balls during the play of a hole, the first to play the wrong ball other than from a hazard shall lose the hole; when this cannot be determined, the hole shall be played out with the balls exchanged. **Rule 15–2.**

Stroke Play

If the competitor plays a stroke with the wrong ball except in a hazard, *he shall add two penalty strokes to his score* for the hole and shall then play the correct ball (provided he has not made a stroke on the next teeing ground, or, in the case of the last hole of the round, has not left the putting green). Strokes played with a wrong ball do not count in his score. **Rule 15–3.**

There is no penalty for a player playing a stroke or strokes in a hazard with a wrong ball provided he then plays the correct ball, in match play and stroke play. Strokes played with a wrong ball do not count in his score. **Rule 15–2, –3.**

THE PUTTING GREEN

TOUCHING LINE OF PUTT

The line of putt must not be touched except:

(i) the player may move sand, loose soil and other loose impediments by picking them up or by brushing them aside with his hand or a club without pressing anything down;

(ii) in addressing the ball, the player may place the club in front of the ball without pressing anything down;

(iii) in measuring—**Rule 10–4**;

(iv) in lifting the ball—**Rule 16–1b**;

(v) in repairing old hole plugs or ball marks—**Rule 16–1c**; and

(vi) in removing movable obstructions—**Rule 24–1**.

(Indicating line for putting on putting green—**Rule 8–2b**.)

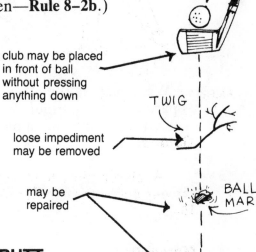

BALL

club may be placed
in front of ball
without pressing
anything down

TWIG

loose impediment
may be removed

may be
repaired

BALL
MARK

HOLE PLUG

may not
be repaired

SPIKE
MARKS

STANDING ASTRIDE OR ON LINE OF PUTT

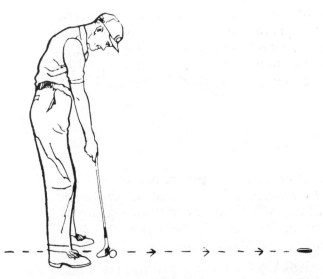

The player shall not make a *stroke* on the *putting green* from a *stance* astride, or with either foot touching, the line of the putt or an extension of that line behind the ball. For the purpose of this Clause only, the line of putt does not extend beyond the hole. **Rule 16–1e.**

POSITION OF CADDIE OR PARTNER

While making the *stroke*, the player shall not allow his caddie, his partner or his partner's caddie to position himself on or close to an extension of the line of putt behind the ball. **Rule 16–1f.**

BALL IN MOTION–OTHER BALL TO BE AT REST

A player shall not play a stroke or touch his ball in play while another ball is in motion after a stroke on the putting green. **Rule 16–1g.**

BALL OVERHANGING HOLE

When any part of the ball overhangs the edge of the hole, the player is allowed enough time to reach the hole without unreasonable delay and an additional 10 seconds to determine whether the ball is at rest. If by then the ball has not fallen into the hole, it is deemed to be at rest. **Rule 16–1h.**

PENALTY for breach of Rule 16–1: *Match play—Loss of hole; Stroke play—Two strokes.*

CONCEDING OPPONENT'S NEXT STROKE

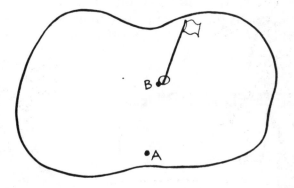

When the opponent's ball is at rest or is deemed to be at rest, the player may concede the opponent to have holed out with his next stroke and the ball may be removed by either side with a club or otherwise. **Rule 16–2.**

THE FLAGSTICK

ATTENDED, REMOVED OR HELD UP

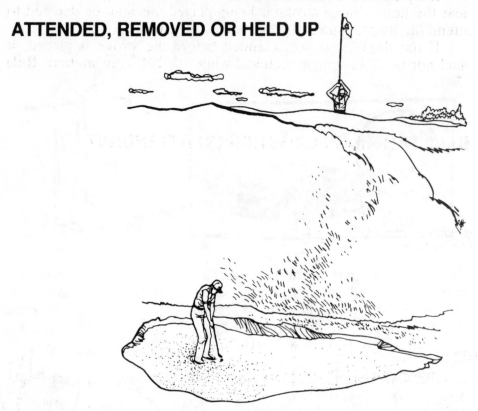

Before and during the *stroke,* the player may have the flagstick attended, removed or held up to indicate the position of the hole. This may be done only on the authority of the player before he plays his stroke.

If the flagstick is attended or removed by an opponent, a fellow-competitor or the caddie of either with the player's knowledge and no objection is made, the player shall be deemed to have authorized it. **Rule 17–1.** PENALTY: *Match play—Loss of hole; Stroke play—Two strokes.*

WHEN DEEMED ATTENDED

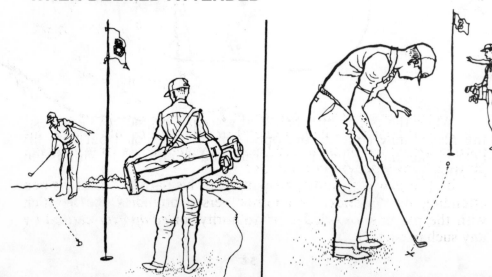

If a player or a caddie attends or removes the flagstick or stands near the hole while a stroke is being played, he shall be deemed to attend the flagstick until the ball comes to rest.

If the flagstick is not attended before the stroke is played, it shall not be attended or removed while the ball is in motion. **Rule 17–1.**

BALL STRIKING FLAGSTICK OR ATTENDANT

*Flagstick Unattended;
Play off Green*

*Flagstick Attended;
Play from or off Green*

The player's ball shall not strike:
a. The flagstick when attended or removed by the player, his partner or either of their caddies, or by another person with the player's knowledge or authority; or
b. The player's caddie, his partner or his partner's caddie when attending the flagstick, or another person attending the flagstick with the player's knowledge or authority, or *equipment* carried by any such person; or

53

Flagstick Unattended;
Play from Green

c. The flagstick in the hole, unattended, when the ball has been played from the *putting green.* **Rule 17–3.** PENALTY for breach of Rule: *Match play—Loss of hole; Stroke play—Two strokes, and the ball shall be played as it lies.*

BALL RESTING AGAINST FLAGSTICK

If the ball rests against the flagstick when it is in the hole, the player or someone authorized by him may move or remove the flagstick and if the ball falls into the hole, the player shall be deemed to have holed out at his last stroke; otherwise, the ball, if *moved,* shall be placed on the lip of the hole, without penalty. **Rule 17–4.**

BALL MOVED OR DEFLECTED

BY OUTSIDE AGENCY

"Drop that ball."

If a ball at rest is moved by an *outside agency,* the player shall incur no penalty and the ball shall be replaced before the player plays another *stroke.* If the ball moved is not immediately recoverable, another ball may be substituted. **Rule 18–1.**

BY PLAYER, PARTNER, CADDIE

When a player's ball is *in play,* if (i) the player, his partner or either of their caddies lifts or moves it, touches it purposely (except with a club in the act of addressing it) or causes it to move except as permitted by a Rule, or (ii) equipment of the player or his partner causes the ball to move, *the player shall incur a penalty stroke.* The ball shall be replaced unless the movement of the ball occurs after the player has begun his swing and he does not discontinue his swing. **Rule 18–2a.**

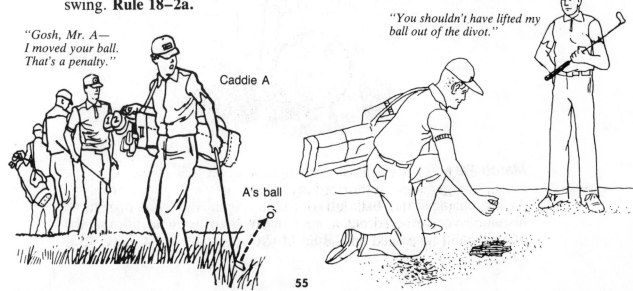

*"Gosh, Mr. A—
I moved your ball.
That's a penalty."*

Caddie A

A's ball

"You shouldn't have lifted my ball out of the divot."

BALL MOVING AFTER ADDRESS

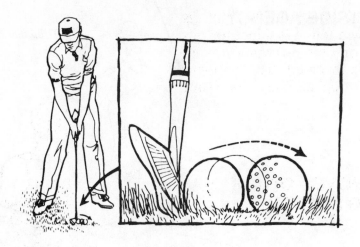

If a *ball in play moves* after the player has *addressed* it other than as a result of a stroke, he shall be deemed to have moved the ball and *shall incur a penalty stroke,* and the ball shall be played as it lies. **Rule 18-2b.**

BALL MOVED BY OPPONENT'S OR FELLOW-COMPETITOR'S SIDE DURING SEARCH

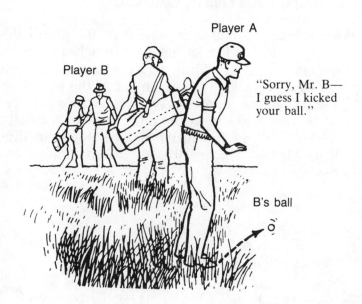

Player A

Player B

"Sorry, Mr. B—
I guess I kicked
your ball."

B's ball

Match Play

If, during search for a player's ball, it is moved by an opponent, his caddie or his *equipment,* no penalty shall be incurred and the player shall replace the ball. **Rule 18-3a.**

Stroke Play

If a competitor's ball is moved by a fellow-competitor, his caddie or his *equipment,* no penalty is incurred. The competitor shall replace his ball. **Rule 18–4.**

BALL MOVED OTHER THAN DURING SEARCH

"Hey, you kicked my ball."

Player B

Player A

B's ball

Match Play

If, other than during search for a ball, the ball is touched or moved by an opponent, his caddie or his *equipment,* except as otherwise provided in the Rules, *the opponent shall incur a penalty stroke.* The player shall replace the ball. **Rule 18–3b.**

Stroke Play

If a competitor's ball is moved by a fellow-competitor, his caddie or his *equipment,* no penalty is incurred. The competitor shall replace his ball. **Rule 18–4.**

BALL MOVED BY ANOTHER BALL

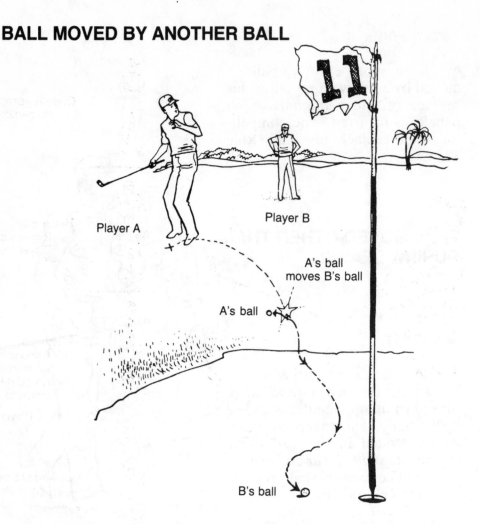

If a player's ball at rest is moved by another ball, the player's ball shall be replaced. **Rule 18–5.** *PENALTY for breach of Rule 18: *Match play—Loss of hole; Stroke play—Two strokes.*

*If a player who is required to replace a ball fails to do so, he shall incur the general penalty for breach of Rule 18 but no additional penalty under Rule 18 shall be applied.

Note: If it is impossible to determine the spot on which a ball is to be placed, see Rule 20–3c.

BALL IN MOTION DEFLECTED OR STOPPED

By Outside Agency

If a ball in motion is accidentally deflected or stopped by any *outside agency,* it is a *rub of the green,* no penalty is incurred, and the ball shall be played as it lies, except:

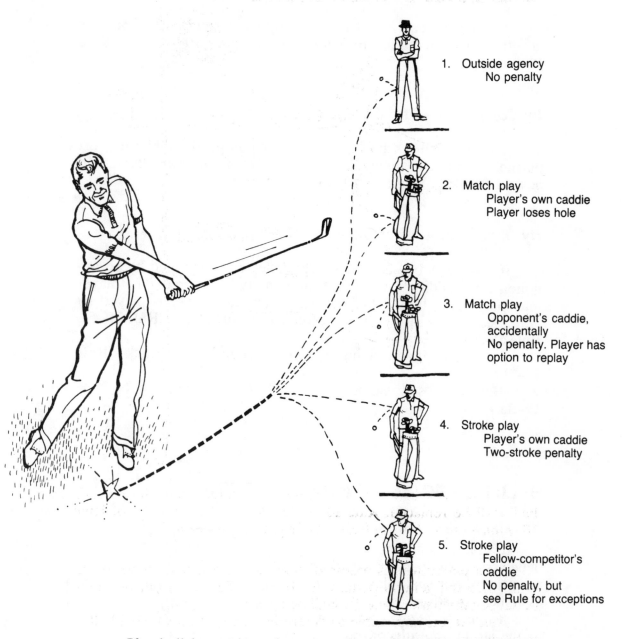

1. Outside agency
   No penalty

2. Match play
   Player's own caddie
   Player loses hole

3. Match play
   Opponent's caddie,
   accidentally
   No penalty. Player has
   option to replay

4. Stroke play
   Player's own caddie
   Two-stroke penalty

5. Stroke play
   Fellow-competitor's
   caddie
   No penalty, but
   see Rule for exceptions

a. If a ball in motion after a *stroke* other than on the *putting green* comes to rest in or on any moving or animate outside agency, the player shall, *through the green* or in a *hazard,* drop the ball, or on the putting green place the ball, as near as possible to the spot where the outside agency was when the ball came to rest in or on it; and

b. If a ball in motion after a stroke on the putting green is deflected or stopped by, or comes to rest in or on, any moving or animate outside agency, the stroke shall be canceled and the ball shall be replaced.

If the ball is not immediately recoverable, another ball may be substituted. **Rule 19–1.**

By Player—Match Play

If a player's ball is deflected or stopped by himself, his partner or either of their caddies or *equipment, he shall lose the hole.* **Rule 19–2a.**

By Competitor—Stroke Play

If a competitor's ball is deflected or stopped by himself, his partner or either of their caddies or *equipment, the competitor shall incur a PENALTY of two strokes.*

By Opponent, Accidentally—Match Play

If a player's ball is accidentally deflected or stopped by an opponent, his caddie or *equipment,* no penalty is incurred. The player may play the ball as it lies or, before another *stroke* is played by either side, cancel the stroke and replay the stroke (see Rule 20–5). **Rule 19–3b.**

Exception: Ball striking person attending a flagstick—**Rule 17–3b**.

(Ball purposely stopped or deflected by opponent—**Rule 19–3a.**)

BALL DEFLECTED BY A BALL AT REST

If a player's ball in motion is deflected or stopped by a ball at rest, the player shall play his ball as it lies. In stroke play, if both balls lay on the *putting green* prior to the stroke, *the player incurs a penalty of two strokes.* Otherwise, no penalty is incurred. **Rule 19–5.**

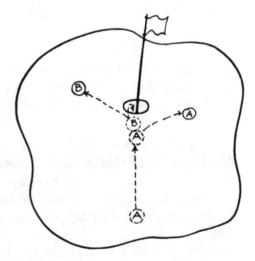

LIFTING, DROPPING AND PLACING; PLAYING FROM A WRONG PLACE

LIFTING

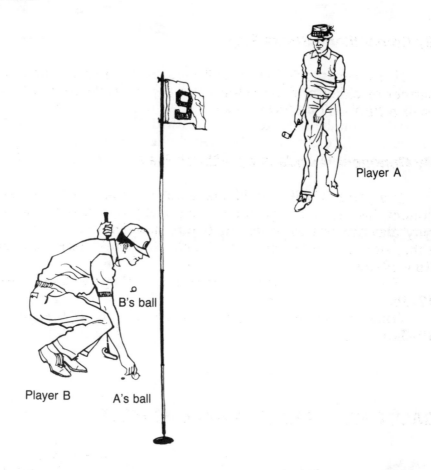

Player A

B's ball

Player B   A's ball

A ball to be lifted under the Rules may be lifted by the player, his partner or another person authorized by the player. In any such case, the player shall be responsible for any breach of the Rules.

BALL TO BE MARKED WHEN LIFTED

The position of the ball shall be marked before it is lifted under a Rule which requires it to be replaced. If it is not marked, the player *shall incur a penalty of one stroke* and the ball shall be replaced. If it is not replaced, the *player shall incur the general penalty* for breach of this Rule but no additional penalty under Rule 20–1 shall be applied.

If a ball is accidentally moved in the process of lifting it under a Rule, no penalty shall be incurred and the ball shall be replaced.

 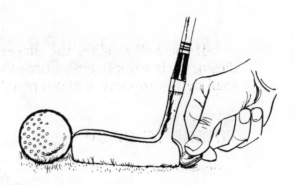

Note: The position of a lifted ball should be marked, if feasible, by placing a ball-marker or other small object immediately behind the ball. If the ball-marker interferes with the play, *stance* or *stroke* of another player, it should be placed one or more clubhead-lengths to one side. **Rule 20–1.**

DROPPING AND RE-DROPPING

By Whom and How

A ball to be dropped under the Rules shall be dropped by the player himself. He shall stand erect, hold the ball at shoulder height and arm's length and drop it. If a ball is dropped by any other person or in any other manner and the error is not corrected as provided in Rule 20–6, *the player shall incur a penalty stroke.*

If the ball touches the player, his partner, either of their caddies or their equipment before or after it strikes the ground, the ball shall be re-dropped, without penalty. **Rule 20–2a.**

WHERE TO DROP

When a ball is to be dropped, it shall be dropped as near as possible to the spot where the ball lay, but not nearer the hole, except when a Rule permits it to be dropped elsewhere. If a ball is to be dropped in a *hazard,* the ball shall be dropped in and come to rest in that hazard. **Rule 20–2b.**

DROPPED BALL ROLLING INTO NEW SITUATION

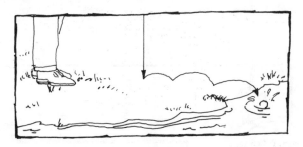

Water hazard

A dropped ball shall be re-dropped without penalty if it rolls (i) into a *hazard;* (ii) out of a hazard; (iii) onto a *putting green;* (iv) *out of bounds;* (v) back into the condition from which relief was taken under Rule 24–2 or Rule 25; (vi) more than two club-lengths from where it first struck the ground; or (vii) comes to rest nearer the hole than is permitted by the Rules.

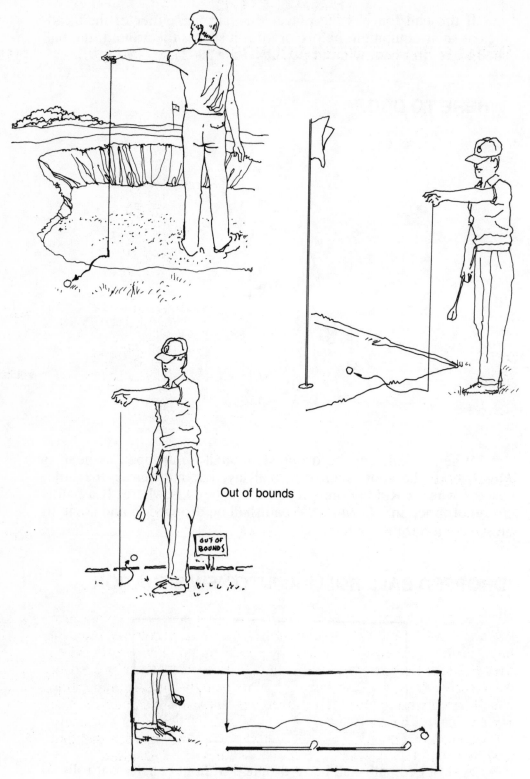

Out of bounds

More than two club-lengths from point of striking ground

If the ball again rolls into such position, it shall be placed as near as possible to the spot where it first struck the ground when re-dropped. **Rule 20–2c.**

PLACING AND REPLACING

How and Where to Place

A ball to be placed under the Rules shall be placed by the player or his partner. A ball to be replaced shall be replaced by the player, his partner or the person who lifted or moved it on the spot where the ball lay. **Rule 20–3a.**

Spot Not Determinable

If it is impossible to determine the spot where the ball is to be placed the ball shall, *through the green* or in a *hazard,* be dropped, or on the *putting green* be placed, as near as possible to the place where it lay but not nearer the hole. **Rule 20–3c.**

Ball Fails to Remain on Spot

If a ball when placed fails to remain on the spot on which it was placed, it shall be replaced without penalty. If it still fails to remain on that spot, it shall be placed at the nearest spot not nearer the hole where it can be placed at rest. **Rule 20–3d.**

Ball in Play When Dropped or Placed

A ball dropped or placed under a Rule governing the particular case is *in play*. **Rule 20–4.**

LIE OF BALL TO BE PLACED OR REPLACED ALTERED

"Please lift your ball. It interferes with me."

B's lie is altered

Player B

A's ball

B's ball

Player A

Player B

Except in a bunker, if the original lie of a ball to be placed or replaced has been altered, the ball shall be placed in the nearest lie most similar to that which it originally occupied, not more than one club-length from the original lie and not nearer the hole. In a bunker, the original lie shall be recreated as nearly as possible and the ball shall be placed in that lie. **Rule 20–3b.** PENALTY for breach of Rule 20–1, –2 or –3: *Match play—Loss of hole; Stroke play—Two strokes.*

PLAYING NEXT STROKE FROM WHERE PREVIOUS STROKE PLAYED

*"I've hit my shot out of bounds.
I'll have to put another ball in play. Do I drop it or place it?"*

"You are through the green, so you drop it."

When, under the Rules, a player elects or is required to play his next *stroke* from where a previous stroke was played, he shall proceed as follows: If the stroke is to be played from the *teeing ground,* the ball to be played shall be played from anywhere within the teeing ground and may be teed; if the stroke is to be played from *through the green* or a *hazard,* it shall be dropped; if the stroke is to be played on the *putting green,* it shall be placed. **Rule 20–5.**

LIFTING BALL WRONGLY DROPPED OR PLACED

A ball dropped or placed in a wrong place or otherwise not in accordance with the Rules but not played may be lifted, without penalty, and the player shall then proceed correctly.

In match play, if, before the opponent plays his next stroke, the player fails to inform him that the ball has been lifted, *the player shall lose the hole.* **Rule 20–6.**

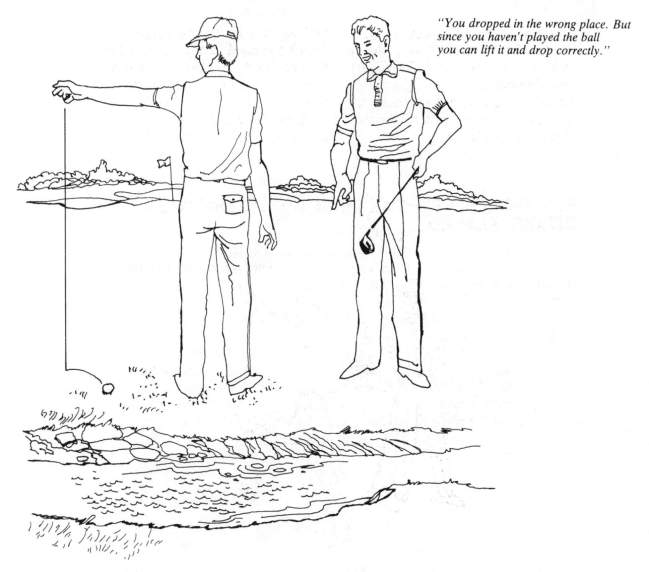

"You dropped in the wrong place. But since you haven't played the ball you can lift it and drop correctly."

CLEANING BALL

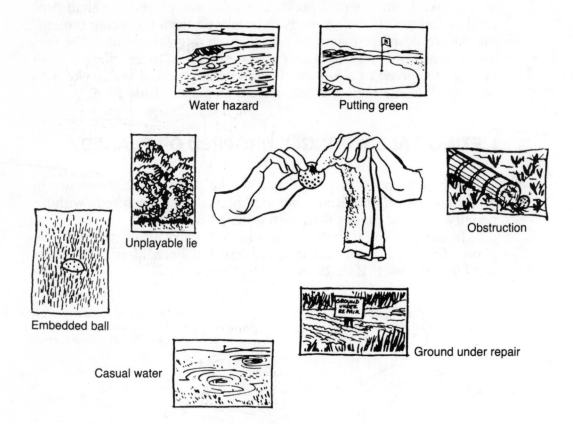

Water hazard

Putting green

Unplayable lie

Obstruction

Embedded ball

Casual water

Ground under repair

A ball may be cleaned when lifted as follows:

Upon suspension of play in accordance with Rule 6–8b;

For identification under Rule 12–2, but the ball may be cleaned only to the extent necessary for identification;

On the *putting green* under Rule 16–1b;

For relief from an *obstruction* under Rule 24–1b or –2b;

For relief from abnormal ground conditions or wrong putting green under Rules 25–1b, –2 and –3;

For relief from a *water hazard* under Rule 26;

For relief for an unplayable ball under Rule 28; or

Under a Local Rule permitting cleaning the ball.

If the player cleans his ball during the play of a hole except as permitted under this Rule, *he shall incur a penalty of one stroke* and the ball, if lifted, shall be replaced.

If a player who is required to replace a ball fails to do so, *he shall incur the general penalty* for breach of Rule 20–3a, but no additional penalty under Rule 21 shall be applied.

BALL INTERFERING WITH OR ASSISTING PLAY

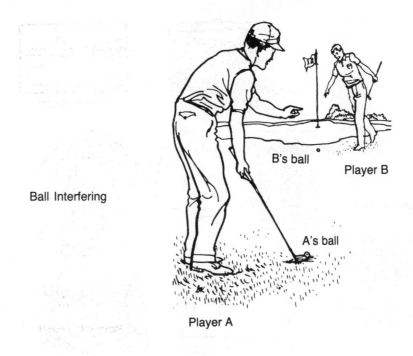

Ball Interfering

B's ball

Player B

A's ball

Player A

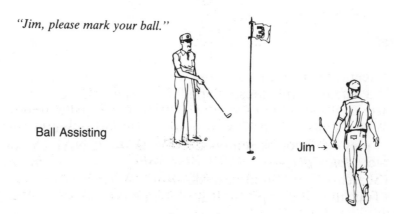

"Jim, please mark your ball."

Ball Assisting

Jim →

Any player may: a) lift his ball if he considers that it might assist any other player, or (b) have any other ball lifted if he considers that it might interfere with his play or assist the play of any other player, but this may not be done while another ball is in motion. In stroke play, a player required to lift his ball may play first rather than lift. A ball lifted under this Rule shall be replaced.

If a ball is accidentally moved in complying with this Rule, no penalty is incurred and the ball shall be replaced.

LOOSE IMPEDIMENTS

May the twig be removed? Yes, but . . . There's a penalty if the ball moves

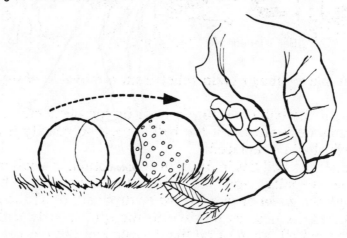

Relief

Except when both the *loose impediment* and the ball lie in or touch a *hazard,* any loose impediment may be removed without penalty.

When a player's ball is in motion, a loose impediment on his line of play shall not be removed. **Rule 23–1.** PENALTY for breach of Rule: *Match play—Loss of hole; Stroke play—Two strokes.*

(Searching for ball in hazard—Rule 12–1.)

(Touching line of putt—Rule 16–1a.)

Ball Moving After Loose Impediment Touched

Through the green, if the ball *moves* after any *loose impediment* lying within a club-length of it has been touched by the player, his partner or either of their caddies and before the player has *addressed* it, the player shall be deemed to have moved the ball and *shall incur a PENALTY stroke.* The player shall replace the ball unless the movement of the ball occurs after the player has begun his swing and he does not discontinue his swing.

On the *putting green,* if the ball moves in the process of removing any *loose impediment,* it shall be replaced without penalty. **Rule 18–2c.**

OBSTRUCTIONS
MOVABLE OBSTRUCTIONS

A player may obtain relief from a movable *obstruction* as follows:

a. If the ball does not lie in or on the obstruction, the obstruction may be removed; if the ball moves, no penalty is incurred and the ball shall be replaced.

b. If the ball lies in or on the obstruction, the ball may be lifted, without penalty, and the obstruction removed. The ball shall *through the green* or in *a hazard* be dropped, or on the *putting green* be placed, as near as possible to the spot directly under the place where the ball lay in or on the obstruction, but not nearer the hole. **Rule 24–1.**

IMMOVABLE OBSTRUCTIONS

Interference by an immovable obstruction occurs when a ball lies in or on the obstruction, or so close to the obstruction that the obstruction interferes with the player's *stance* or the area of his intended swing. A player may obtain relief from interference by an immovable *obstruction,* without penalty, as follows:

(i) *Through the green,* the point nearest to where the ball lies shall be determined (without crossing over, through or under the obstruction) which (1) is not nearer the hole, (2) avoids interference (as defined), and (3) is not in a *hazard* or on a *putting green.* The player shall lift the ball and drop it within one club-length of the point thus determined on ground which fulfills (1), (2) and (3) above.

Note: The prohibition against crossing over, through or under the *obstruction* does not apply to the artificial surfaces and sides of roads and paths or when the ball lies in or on the obstruction.

(ii) *In a bunker,* the player shall lift and drop the ball in accordance with Clause (i) above, except that the ball must be dropped in the *bunker.*

(iii) *On the putting green,* the player shall lift and place the ball in the nearest position to where it lay which affords relief from interference, but not nearer the hole nor in a hazard.

Exception: A player may not obtain relief under Rule 24–2b if (a) it is clearly unreasonable for him to play a stroke because of interference by any thing other than an immovable obstruction or (b) interference by an immovable obstruction would occur only through use of an unnecessarily abnormal stance, swing or direction of play.

Note: If a ball lies in or touches a *water hazard* (including a *lateral water hazard*), the player is not entitled to relief without penalty from interference by an immovable obstruction. The player shall play the ball as it lies or proceed under Rule 26–1. **Rule 24–2b.** PENALTY for breach of Rule: *Match play—Loss of hole; Stroke play—Two strokes.*

RELIEF FROM PAVED CART PATH

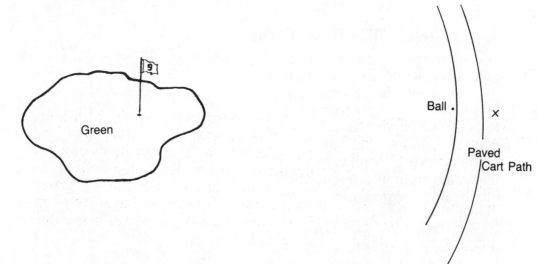

The ball is in such position that the paved cart path (an obstruction) interferes with the player's stance. Although Rule 24–2b in general prohibits crossing over the obstruction in determining the nearest point of relief, the prohibition does not apply to paved paths—(see Note). Thus, the player, if he desires relief, must drop the ball within one club-length of point X, the nearest point of relief not nearer the hole.

NO RELIEF FOR LINE OF PLAY ALONE

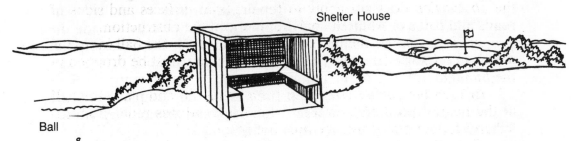

The ball lies so far behind the shelter house that it does not interfere with the player's swing. The player is not entitled to drop his ball so as to avoid the shelter house on line to the green. Rule 24–2a provides in these circumstances that intervention on the line of play is not, of itself, interference under this Rule.

ABNORMAL GROUND CONDITIONS AND WRONG PUTTING GREEN

RELIEF FROM CASUAL WATER OR GROUND UNDER REPAIR

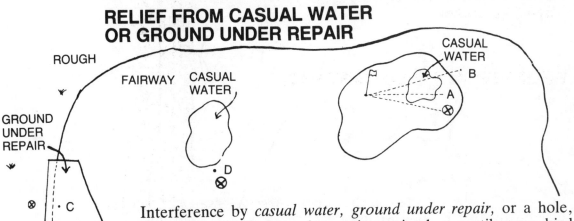

Interference by *casual water, ground under repair,* or a hole, cast or runway made by a burrowing animal, a reptile or a bird occurs when a ball lies in or touches any of these conditions or when the condition interferes with the player's stance or the area of his intended swing. If the player's ball lies on the *putting green,* interference also occurs if such condition or the putting green intervenes on his line of putt. If interference exists, the player may either play the ball as it lies or take relief as follows:

On the Putting Green

Ball A lies on the putting green with casual water intervening between it and the hole. *Ball A* may be lifted without penalty and placed at nearby point X, which is the nearest position to where it lay which affords maximum relief from the casual water, but not nearer the hole. (If *Ball A* were lying *in* casual water on the putting green, similar relief would be available.) **Rule 25–1b (iii).**

Ball B lies off the putting green. The player is not entitled to relief from casual water lying on the putting green which intervenes between *Ball B* and the hole.

Ball C lies in ground under repair, in an area normally "fairway." *Ball C* may be lifted and dropped without penalty outside the ground under repair within one club-length of X, the nearest point which (a) is not nearer the hole, (b) avoids interference by the condition, and (c) is not in a hazard or on a putting green. **Rule 25–1b(i).** (The permissible drop area is in the "rough," but the Rules do not distinguish between "fairway" and "rough"—both are "through the green," according to definition.)

Ball D lies so near to casual water that a right-handed player would be obliged to stand in casual water. He may lift and drop the ball without penalty outside the casual water, within one club-length of the nearest point of relief not nearer the hole. The point is indicated by the X.

PENALTY for breach of Rule: *Match play—Loss of hole; Stroke play—Two strokes.*

CASUAL WATER IN BUNKER

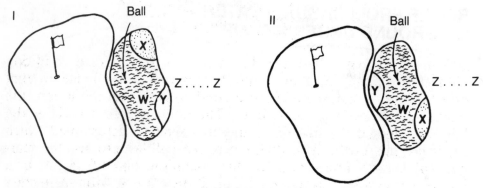

Area W—water three inches deep; *Area X*—water one-eighth inch deep; *Area Y*—no casual water.

I. The player would like to drop the ball in area X. However, he may drop only:
1. At nearest point in area Y, without penalty, or
2. Along line Z . . . Z behind the bunker, under penalty of one stroke.

II. The player may drop the ball at either:
1. The nearest point in area X, without penalty, or
2. Along line Z . . . Z behind the bunker, under penalty of one stroke. He may not drop in area Y as it is nearer the hole than the ball's original position.

In a bunker, if there is interference by casual water, ground under repair, or a hole, cast or runway made by a burrowing animal, a reptile or a bird, the player may lift and drop the ball either:

Without penalty, in the bunker as near as possible to the spot where his ball lay, but not nearer the hole, on ground which affords maximum relief from the condition;

or

Under penalty of one stroke, outside the bunker, keeping the spot where his ball lay directly between himself and the hole.

PENALTY for breach of Rule: *Match play—Loss of hole; Stroke play—Two strokes.* **Rule 25–1b(ii).**

BALL LOST IN CASUAL WATER OR GROUND UNDER REPAIR

"I'm sure my ball went in here, but I can't find it."

In order that a ball may be treated as lost under a condition covered by Rule 25, there must be reasonable evidence to that effect. If a ball is lost under such condition through the green, the player may take relief as follows: The point nearest to where the ball last crossed the margin of the area shall be determined which (a) is not nearer the hole than where the ball last crossed the margin, (b) avoids interference by the condition, and (c) is not in a hazard or on a putting green. He shall drop a ball without penalty within one club-length of the point thus determined on ground which fulfills (a), (b) and (c) above. **Rule 25–1c.** PENALTY for breach of Rule: *Match play—Loss of hole; Stroke play—Two strokes.*

EMBEDDED BALL

Ball in fairway

Ball in rough

A ball embedded in its own pitch-mark in any closely mown area *through the green* may be lifted, cleaned and dropped, without penalty, as near as possible to the spot where it lay but not nearer the hole. "Closely mown area" means any area of the *course,* including paths through the rough, cut to fairway height or less. **Rule 25–2.**

BALL ON A WRONG PUTTING GREEN

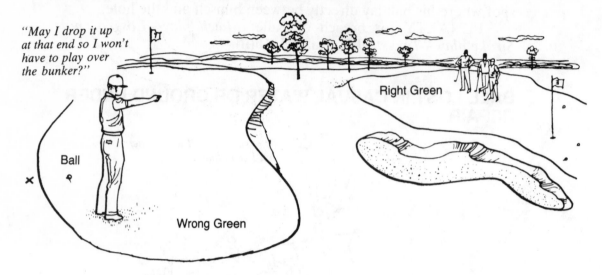

"May I drop it up at that end so I won't have to play over the bunker?"

If a ball lies on a *putting green* other than that of the hole being played, the point on the *course* nearest to where the ball lies shall be determined which (a) is not nearer the hole and (b) is not in a *hazard* or on a putting green. The player shall lift the ball and drop it without penalty within one club-length of the point thus determined on ground which fulfills (a) and (b) above. In the illustration, the player must drop off the green within one club-length of point X.

WATER HAZARDS (INCLUDING LATERAL WATER HAZARDS)

BALL IN WATER HAZARD—PROCEDURE

Player T's ball lies in the water hazard in front of green. He may drop a ball, under penalty of one stroke, either:

a. Behind the water hazard, keeping the spot (C) at which the ball last crossed the margin of the water hazard between himself and the hole, and with no limit to how far behind the water hazard the ball may be dropped (the line of dropping is X—X—X—X);

or

b. As near as possible to the spot from which the original ball was played; if the stroke was played from the teeing ground, the ball may be teed anywhere within the teeing ground. **Rule 26–1.**

Player Q's ball has entered the lateral water hazard at left. He may, under penalty of one stroke, either:

a. Drop a ball behind the lateral water hazard, keeping the spot (D) at which the ball crossed the margin of the lateral water hazard between himself and the hole (the line of dropping is Z—Z—Z—Z);

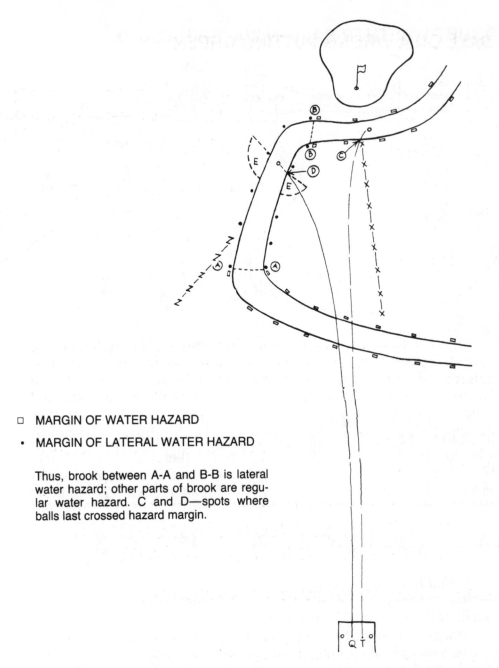

□ MARGIN OF WATER HAZARD

• MARGIN OF LATERAL WATER HAZARD

Thus, brook between A-A and B-B is lateral water hazard; other parts of brook are regular water hazard. C and D—spots where balls last crossed hazard margin.

or

b. Drop a ball as near as possible to the spot from which the original ball was played; if the stroke was played from the teeing ground, the ball may be teed anywhere within the teeing ground;

or

c. Drop a ball outside the hazard within two club-lengths of the point (D) where the ball last crossed the hazard margin or a point on the opposite margin of the hazard equidistant from the hole. The ball must be dropped and come to rest not nearer the hole than point D. Thus, Player Q may drop a ball on either area marked E. **Rule 26–1.**

PENALTY for breach of Rule: *Match play—Loss of hole; Stroke play—Two strokes.*

DOUBT WHETHER BALL IN WATER HAZARD

"If my ball is lost in the water hazard, I can save distance."

It is a question of fact whether a ball lost after having been struck toward a water hazard is lost inside or outside the hazard. In order to treat the ball as lost in the hazard, there must be reasonable evidence that the ball lodged therein. In the absence of such evidence, the ball must be treated as a lost ball and Rule 27 applies.

BALL PLAYED WITHIN WATER HAZARD

a. *Ball Remains in Hazard*

If a ball played from within a water hazard has not crossed any margin of the hazard, the player may:

(i) proceed under Rule 26–1; or

(ii) *under penalty of one stroke,* play his next stroke as nearly as possible at the spot from which the last stroke from outside the hazard was played (see Rule 20–5).

b. *Ball Lost or Unplayable Outside Hazard or Out of Bounds*

If a ball played from within a water hazard is lost or declared unplayable outside the hazard or is out of bounds, the player, after taking a stroke-and-distance penalty under Rule 27–1 or 28a, may:

(i) play a ball as nearly as possible at the spot from which the original ball was last played by him (see Rule 20–5); or

(ii) under the penalty prescribed therein, proceed under Rule 26–1b or, as additional options in the case of a lateral water hazard, under Rule 26–1c, using as the reference point the point where the ball last crossed the margin of the hazard before it came to rest in the hazard; or

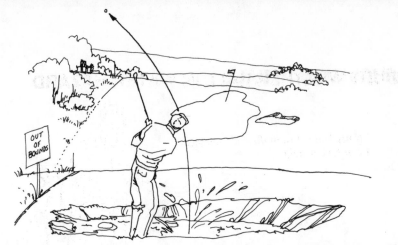

(iii) *under penalty of one stroke,* play his next stroke as nearly as possible at the spot from which the last stroke from outside the hazard was played (see Rule 20–5).

Rule 26–2. PENALTY for breach of Rule: *Match play—Loss of hole; Stroke play—Two strokes.*

BALL LOST; OUT OF BOUNDS; OR UNPLAYABLE

BALL LOST OR OUT OF BOUNDS

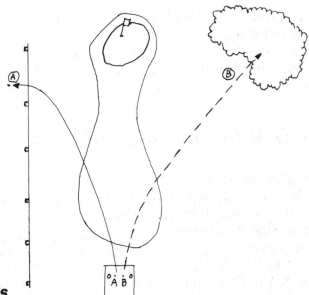

Out of Bounds

Player A's ball is out of bounds. He must replay from the tee, count both strokes made and add a penalty stroke to his score for the hole. **Rule 27–1.**

Lost

Player B is unable to find his ball in the thick underbrush. His only procedure for a lost ball is to play again from the tee, count both strokes played and add a penalty stroke to his score for the hole. **Rule 27–1.**

PROVISIONAL BALL

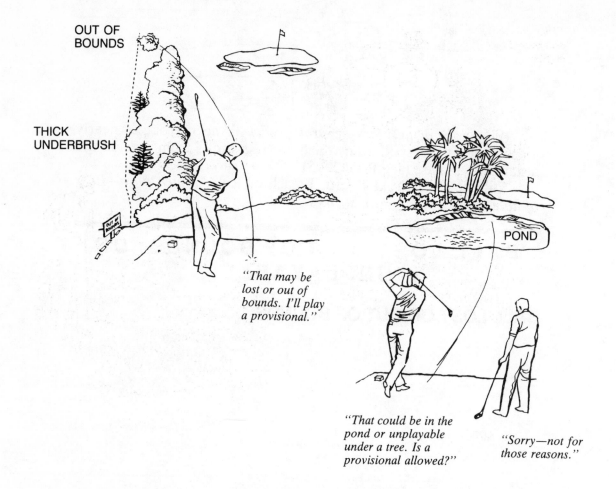

OUT OF
BOUNDS

THICK
UNDERBRUSH

"That may be lost or out of bounds. I'll play a provisional."

POND

"That could be in the pond or unplayable under a tree. Is a provisional allowed?"

"Sorry—not for those reasons."

If a ball may be *lost* outside a *water hazard* or may be *out of bounds,* to save time the player may play another ball provisionally as nearly as possible at the spot from which the original ball was played—see Rule 20–5. The player shall inform his opponent in match play or his marker or a fellow-competitor in stroke play that he intends to play a *provisional ball,* and he shall play it before he or his partner goes forward to search for the original ball. If he fails to do so, and plays another ball, such ball is not a provisional ball and becomes the *ball in play* under penalty of stroke and distance (Rule 27–1); the original ball is deemed to be lost.

PENALTY for breach of Rule: *Match play—Loss of hole; Stroke play—Two strokes.* **Rule 27–2.**

WHEN PROVISIONAL BALL BECOMES BALL IN PLAY

"That puts the provisional ball in play."

Original ball

Provisional ball

"That's unplayable. I'll have to give up the provisional ball, too."

Original ball

Provisional ball

The player may play a provisional ball until he reaches the place where the original ball is likely to be. If he plays a stroke with the provisional ball from the place where the original ball is likely to be or from a point nearer the hole than that place, the original ball is deemed to be *lost,* and the provisional ball becomes the ball in play *under penalty of stroke and distance.*

If the original ball is lost outside a water hazard or is out of bounds, the provisional ball becomes the ball in play, *under penalty of stroke and distance* (Rule 27–1). **Rule 27–2b.**

If the original ball is neither lost outside a water hazard nor out of bounds, the player shall abandon the provisional ball and continue play with the original ball. If he fails to do so, any further strokes played with the provisional ball shall constitute playing a *wrong ball* and the provisions of Rule 15 shall apply. **Rule 27–2c.**

Note: If the original ball lies in a water hazard, the player shall play the ball as it lies or proceed under Rule 26. If it is lost in a water hazard or unplayable, the player shall proceed under Rule 26 or 28, whichever is applicable.

BALL UNPLAYABLE

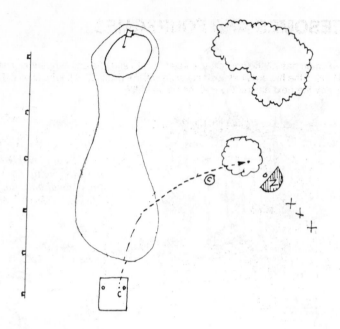

Player C finds his ball at the base of a thick, bushy tree. He declares it unplayable under Rule 28 (the player may declare it unplayable at any place on the course except in a water hazard). He has three options for relief:

1. He may play again from the tee under penalty of one stroke (see Rule 20–5).

2. He may drop a ball, under penalty of one stroke, either:

(a) Within two club-lengths of the point where the ball lay, but not nearer the hole (shaded area Z), or

(b) Behind the unplayable lie on line XXX so as to keep the point where the ball lies unplayable between himself and the hole, with no limit to how far behind that point the ball may be dropped. (If the ball lies in a bunker and Player C elects to proceed under option 2(a) or 2(b), he would have to drop in the bunker.) **Rule 28.**

PENALTY for breach of Rule: *Match play—Loss of hole; Stroke play—Two strokes.*

OTHER FORMS OF PLAY

THREESOMES AND FOURSOMES

The women has hit the ball into the water hazard and she and her partner wish to drop a ball behind the hazard under penalty of one stroke (Rule 26–1). Who should drop the ball and play the next stroke, the man or his partner?

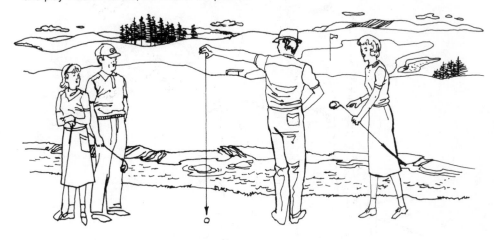

The man must play the next stroke because a penalty stroke does not affect the order of play.

General

In a threesome or a foursome, during any *stipulated round* the partners shall play alternately from the teeing grounds and alternately during the play of each hole. *Penalty strokes* do not affect the order of play. **Rule 29–1.**

Match Play

If a player plays when his partner should have played, *his side shall lose the hole*. **Rule 29–2.**

Stroke Play

If the partners play a stroke or strokes in incorrect order, such stroke or strokes shall be canceled, and *the side shall be penalized two strokes*. A ball shall then be put in play as nearly as possible at the spot from which the side first played in incorrect order (see Rule 20–5) before a stroke has been played from the next *teeing ground*, or, in the case of the last hole of the round, before the side has left the *putting green*. If this is not done, *the side shall be disqualified*. **Rule 29–3.**

FOUR-BALL MATCH AND STROKE PLAY

"My partner's not here, so I'll represent our side."

Representation of Side

A side may be represented by one partner for all or any part of a match or stipulated round; all partners need not be present. An absent partner may join a match between holes, but not during play of a hole. **Rules 30–3a** and **31–2.**

ORDER OF PLAY

"You putt first, partner, so I can get some idea about the line."

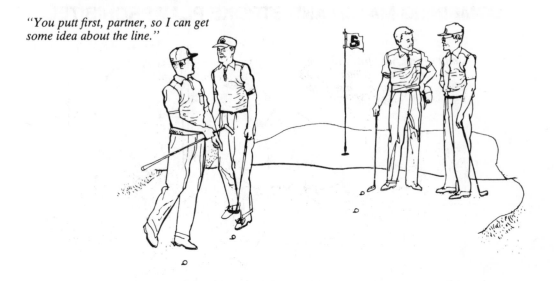

Match Play and Stroke Play

Balls belonging to the same side may be played in the order the side considers best. **Rules 30–3c** and **31–5.**

BREACH AFFECTING OTHER PLAYER

"You're not allowed to remove impediment in a hazard. We are both penalized."

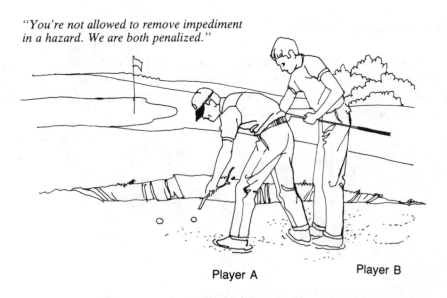

Player A   Player B

If a player's breach of a Rule assists his partner's play, or in match play adversely affects an opponent's play, *the partner incurs the relative penalty in addition to any penalty incurred by the player.* **Rules 30–3f** and **31–8.**

THE COMMITTEE

COMBINING MATCH AND STROKE PLAY PROHIBITED

"Can't we kill two birds with one stone today—play our match in the club championship and also compete in the weekly medal play?"

"No—it wouldn't be right."

Certain special rules governing stroke play are so substantially different from those governing match play that combining the two forms of play is not practicable and is not permitted. The results of matches played and the scores returned in these circumstances shall not be accepted. **Rule 33–1.**

DEFINING BOUNDS AND MARGINS

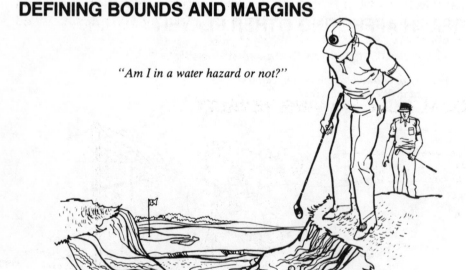

"Am I in a water hazard or not?"

The Committee shall define accurately:
a. The *course* and *out of bounds.*
b. The margins of *water hazards* and *lateral water hazards.*
c. *Ground under repair.*
d. *Obstructions and integral parts of the course.* **Rule 33–2a.**

COURSE UNPLAYABLE

If the Committee or its authorized representative considers that for any reason the course is not in a playable condition or that there are circumstances which render the proper playing of the game impossible, it may, in match or stroke play, order a temporary suspension of play or, in stroke play, declare play null and void and cancel all scores for the round in question.

When play has been temporarily suspended, it shall be resumed from where it was discontinued, even though resumption occurs on a subsequent day. When a round is canceled, all penalties incurred in that round are canceled. **Rule 33–2d.**

(Procedure in discontinuing play—Rule 6–8.)

LOCAL RULE WAIVING PENALTY

"There's a Local Rule here—no penalty for dropping out of a water hazard. That's wrong."

A penalty imposed by a Rule of Golf shall not be waived by a Local Rule. **Rule 33–8b.**

This book contains a complete recodification of the Rules of Golf. The Rules have been rearranged, renumbered and in many cases re-written. In addition, a number of substantive changes have been made, the most important of which are summarized on pages 123-126.

To familiarize yourself with the new Rules book, first study the Table of Contents at the front to get an idea of how the Rules are now organized. Then look at the captions under each Rule to see the matters covered and the order in which they are treated. Having done this, it is hoped that most of the time you will be able to find the relevant Rule simply by reference to the Table of Contents. If not, there is an Index on pages 111-122 which should lead you to the relevant Rule.

The following suggestions are offered for learning how to apply the Rules of Golf to specific cases:

1. Identify the form of play. Match play or stroke play? The penalties differ significantly. Single, foursome or four-ball? (A foursome and a four-ball are not the same thing.) Singles match play and individual stroke play are covered in Rules 1-28. These Rules, as supplemented and modified by Rules 29-32, govern threesomes and foursomes, multi-ball match play and stroke play and bogey, par and Stableford competitions.

2. Who is involved? The player, his partner or his caddie? In match play, the player's opponent or his caddie? In stroke play, a fellow-competitor or his caddie? Or an outside agency?

3. Where did the incident occur? On the teeing ground of the hole being played? In a hazard (*i.e.*, a bunker, a water hazard or a lateral water hazard)? On the putting green of the hole being played? Or elsewhere on the course (*i.e.*, "through the green")? Where the incident occurs can have a significant effect on what the player may do or the relief to which he is entitled.

4. Pay attention to the Definitions set forth in full in alphabetical order at the front of the book. Definitions are repeated at the beginning of each Rule in which they are used and are likely to be important to the correct application of the Rule. Defined terms which may be significant are underscored the first time they appear in a Rule.

5. Carry a Rules book in your golf bag and use it whenever a question arises. Knowing the Rules may enable you not only to avoid penalties but also to save strokes.

THE RULES OF GOLF

Section I
ETIQUETTE

Courtesy on the Course
Consideration for Other Players

The player who has the honor should be allowed to play before his opponent or fellow-competitor tees his ball.

No one should move, talk or stand close to or directly behind the ball or the hole when a player is addressing the ball or making a stroke.

In the interest of all, players should play without delay.

No player should play until the players in front are out of range.

Players searching for a ball should signal the players behind them to pass as soon as it becomes apparent that the ball will not easily be found. They should not search for five minutes before doing so. They should not continue play until the players following them have passed and are out of range.

When the play of a hole has been completed, players should immediately leave the putting green.

Priority on the Course

In the absence of special rules, two-ball matches should have precedence over and be entitled to pass any three- or four-ball match.

A single player has no standing and should give way to a match of any kind.

Any match playing a whole round is entitled to pass a match playing a shorter round.

If a match fails to keep its place on the course and loses more than one clear hole on the players in front, it should allow the match following to pass.

Care of the Course
Holes in Bunkers

Before leaving a bunker, a player should carefully fill up and smooth over all holes and footprints made by him.

Replace Divots; Repair Ball-Marks and Damage by Spikes

Through the green, a player should ensure that any turf cut or displaced by him is replaced at once and pressed down and that any damage to the putting green made by a ball is carefully repaired. Damage to the putting green caused by golf shoe spikes should be repaired *on completion of the hole.*

Damage to Greens — Flagsticks, Bags, etc.

Players should ensure that, when putting down bags or the flagstick, no damage is done to the putting green and that neither they nor their caddies damage the hole by standing close to it, in handling the flagstick or in removing the ball from the hole. The flagstick should be properly replaced in the hole before the players leave the putting green. Players should not damage the putting green by leaning on their putters, particularly when removing the ball from the hole.

Golf Carts

Local notices regulating the movement of golf carts should be strictly observed.

Damage Through Practice Swings

In taking practice swings, players should avoid causing damage to the course, particularly the tees, by removing divots.

Section II
DEFINITIONS

Addressing the Ball

A player has "addressed the ball" when he has taken his stance and has also grounded his club, except that in a hazard a player has addressed the ball when he has taken his stance.

Advice

"Advice" is any counsel or suggestion which could influence a player in determining his play, the choice of a club or the method of making a stroke.

Information on the Rules or on matters of public information, such as the position of hazards or the flagstick on the putting green, is not advice.

Ball Deemed to Move

See "Move or Moved."

Ball Holed

See "Holed."

Ball Lost

See "Lost Ball."

Ball in Play

A ball is "in play" as soon as the player has made a stroke on the teeing ground. It remains in play until holed out, except when it is out of bounds, lost or lifted, or another ball has been substituted under an applicable Rule; a ball so substituted becomes the ball in play.

Bunker

A "bunker" is a hazard consisting of a prepared area of ground, often a hollow, from which turf or soil has been removed and replaced with sand or the like. Grass-covered ground bordering or within a bunker is not part of the bunker.

Caddie

A "caddie" is one who carries or handles a player's clubs during play and otherwise assists him in accordance with the Rules.

When one caddie is employed by more than one player, he is always deemed to be the caddie of the player whose ball is involved, and equipment carried by him is deemed to be that player's equipment, except when the caddie acts upon specific directions of another player, in which case he is considered to be that other player's caddie.

Casual Water

"Casual water" is any temporary accumulation of water on the course which is visible before or after the player takes his stance and is not in a water hazard. Snow and ice are either casual water or loose impediments, at the option of the player. Dew is not casual water.

Committee

The "Committee" is the committee in charge of the competition or, if the matter does not arise in a competition, the committee in charge of the course.

Competitor

A "competitor" is a player in a stroke competition. A "fellow-competitor" is any person with whom the competitor plays. Neither is partner of the other.

In stroke play foursome and four-ball competitions, where the context so admits, the word "competitor" or "fellow-competitor" shall be held to include his partner.

Course

The "course" is the whole area within which play is permitted. See Rule 33-2.

Equipment

"Equipment" is anything used, worn or carried by or for the player except any ball he has played and any small object, such as a coin or a tee, when used to mark the position of a ball or the extent of an area in which a ball is to be dropped. Equipment includes a golf cart, whether or not motorized. If such a cart is shared by more than one player, its status under the Rules is the same as that of a caddie employed by more than one player. See "Caddie."

Fellow-Competitor

See "Competitor."

Flagstick

The "flagstick" is a movable straight indicator, with or without bunting or other material attached, centered in the hole to show its position. It shall be circular in cross-section.

Forecaddie

A "forecaddie" is one who is employed by the Committee to indicate to players the position of balls on the course, and is an outside agency.

Ground Under Repair

"Ground under repair" is any portion of the course so marked by order of the Committee or so declared by its authorized representative. It includes material piled for removal and a hole made by a greenkeeper, even if not so marked. Stakes and lines defining ground under repair are in such ground.

Note 1: Grass cuttings and other material left on the course which have been abandoned and are not intended to be removed are not ground under repair unless so marked.

Note 2: The Committee may make a Local Rule prohibiting play from ground under repair.

Hazards

A "hazard" is any bunker or water hazard.

Hole

The "hole" shall be 4¼ inches (108mm) in diameter and at least 4 inches (100mm) deep. If a lining is used, it shall be sunk at least 1 inch (25mm) below the putting green surface unless the nature of the soil makes it impracticable to do so; its outer diameter shall not exceed 4¼ inches (108mm).

Holed

A ball is "holed" when it is at rest within the circumference of the hole and all of it is below the level of the lip of the hole.

Honor

The side entitled to play first from the teeing ground is said to have the "honor."

Lateral Water Hazard

A "lateral water hazard" is a water hazard or that part of a water hazard so situated that it is not possible or is deemed by the Committee to be impracticable to drop a ball behind the water hazard and keep the spot at which the ball last crossed the margin of the water hazard between the player and the hole.

That part of a water hazard to be played as a lateral water hazard should be distinctively marked.

Note: Lateral water hazards should be defined by red stakes or lines.

Loose Impediments

"Loose impediments" are natural objects such as stones, leaves, twigs, branches and the like, dung, worms and insects and casts or heaps made by them, provided they are not fixed or growing, are not solidly embedded and do not adhere to the ball.

Sand and loose soil are loose impediments on the putting green, but not elsewhere.

Snow and ice are either casual water or loose impediments, at the option of the player.

Dew is not a loose impediment.

Lost Ball

A ball is "lost" if:

a. It is not found or identified as his by the player within five minutes after the player's side or his or their caddies have begun to search for it; or

b. The player has put another ball into play under the Rules, even though he may not have searched for the original ball; or

c. The player has played any stroke with a provisional ball from the place where the original ball is likely to be or from a point nearer the hole than that place, whereupon the provisional ball becomes the ball in play.

Time spent in playing a wrong ball is not counted in the five-minute period allowed for search.

Marker

A "marker" is one who is appointed by the Committee to record a competitor's score in stroke play. He may be a fellow-competitor. He is not a referee.

A marker should not lift a ball or mark its position unless authorized to do so by the competitor and, unless he is a fellow-competitor, should not attend the flagstick or stand at the hole or mark its position.

Matches

See "Sides and Matches."

Move or Moved

A ball is deemed to have "moved" if it leaves its position and comes to rest in any other place.

Observer

An "observer" is one who is appointed by the Committee to assist a referee to decide questions of fact and to report to him any breach of a Rule. An observer should not attend the flagstick, stand at or mark the position of the hole, or lift the ball or mark its position.

Obstructions

An "obstruction" is anything artificial, including the artificial surfaces and sides of roads and paths, except:

a. Objects defining out of bounds, such as walls, fences, stakes and railings;

b. Any part of an immovable artificial object which is out of bounds; and

c. Any construction declared by the Committee to be an integral part of the course.

Out of Bounds

"Out of bounds" is ground on which play is prohibited.

When out of bounds is defined by reference to stakes or a fence or as being beyond stakes or a fence, the out of bounds line is determined by the nearest inside points of the stakes or fence posts at ground level excluding angled supports.

When out of bounds is defined by a line on the ground, the line itself is out of bounds.

The out of bounds line is deemed to extend vertically upwards and downwards.

A ball is out of bounds when all of it lies out of bounds.

A player may stand out of bounds to play a ball lying within bounds.

Outside Agency

An "outside agency" is any agency not part of the match or, in stroke play, not part of a competitor's side, and includes a referee, a marker, an observer or a fore-caddie. Neither wind nor water is an outside agency.

Partner

A "partner" is a player associated with another player on the same side.

In a threesome, foursome or a four-ball match where the context so admits, the word "player" shall be held to include his partner.

Penalty Stroke

A "penalty stroke" is one added to the score of a player or side under certain Rules. In a threesome or foursome, penalty strokes do not affect the order of play.

Provisional Ball

A "provisional ball" is a ball played under Rule 27-2 for a ball which may be lost outside a water hazard or may be out of bounds. It ceases to be a provisional ball when the Rule provides either that the player continue play with it as the ball in play or that it be abandoned.

Putting Green

The "putting green" is all ground of the hole being played which is specially prepared for putting or otherwise defined as such by the Committee. A ball is on the putting green when any part of it touches the putting green.

Referee

A "referee" is one who is appointed by the Committee to accompany players to decide questions of fact and apply the Rules of Golf. He shall act on any breach of a Rule which he observes or is reported to him.

A referee should not attend the flagstick, stand at or mark the position of the hole, or lift the ball or mark its position.

Rub of the Green

A "rub of the green" occurs when a ball in motion is accidentally deflected or stopped by any outside agency (see Rule 19-1).

Rule

The term "Rule" includes Local Rules made by the Committee under Rule 33-8a.

Sides and Matches

Side: A player, or two or more players who are partners.

Single: A match in which one plays against another.

Threesome: A match in which one plays against two, and each side plays one ball.

Foursome: A match in which two play against two, and each side plays one ball.

Three-Ball: A match in which three play against one another, each playing his own ball.

Best-Ball: A match in which one plays against the better ball of two or the best ball of three players.

Four-Ball: A match in which two play their better ball against the better ball of two other players.

Stance

Taking the "stance" consists in a player placing his feet in position for and preparatory to making a stroke.

Stipulated Round

The "stipulated round" consists of playing the holes of the course in their correct sequence unless otherwise authorized by the Committee. The number of holes in a stipulated round is 18 unless a smaller number is authorized by the Committee. As to extension of stipulated round in match play, see Rule 2-4.

Stroke

A "stroke" is the forward movement of the club made with the intention of fairly striking at and moving the ball.

Teeing Ground

The "teeing ground" is the starting place for the hole to be played. It is a rectangular area two club-lengths in depth, the front and the sides of which are defined by the outside limits of two tee-markers. A ball is outside the teeing ground when all of it lies outside the teeing ground.

Through the Green

"Through the green" is the whole area of the course except: a. The teeing ground and putting green of the hole being played; and
b. All hazards on the course.

Water Hazard

A "water hazard" is any sea, lake, pond, river, ditch, surface drainage ditch or other open water course (whether or not containing water) and anything of a similar nature.

All ground or water within the margin of a water hazard is part of the water hazard. The margin of a water hazard is deemed to extend vertically upwards. Stakes and lines defining the margins of water hazards are in the hazards.

Note: Water hazards (other than lateral water hazards) should be defined by yellow stakes or lines.

Wrong Ball

A "wrong ball" is any ball other than:
a. The ball in play,
b. A provisional ball or
c. In stroke play, a second ball played under Rule 3-3 or Rule 20-7b.

Section III
THE RULES OF PLAY

THE GAME
Rule 1. The Game

1-1. General

The Game of Golf consists in playing a ball from the teeing ground into the hole by a stroke or successive strokes in accordance with the Rules.

PENALTY FOR BREACH OF RULE 1-1:
Match play — Loss of hole; Stroke play — Disqualification.

1-2. Exerting Influence on Ball

No player or caddie shall take any action to influence the position or the movement of a ball except in accordance with the Rules.

PENALTY FOR BREACH OF RULE 1-2:
Match play — Loss of hole; Stroke play — Two strokes.

Note: In the case of a serious breach of Rule 1-2, the Committee may impose a penalty of disqualification.

1-3. Agreement to Waive Rules

Players shall not agree to exclude the operation of any Rule or to waive any penalty incurred.

PENALTY FOR BREACH OF RULE 1-3:
Match play — Disqualification of both sides; Stroke play — Disqualification of competitors concerned.

1-4. Points Not Covered by Rules

If any point in dispute is not covered by the Rules, the decision shall be made in accordance with equity.

Rule 2. Match Play

2-1. Winner of Hole

In match play the game is played by holes.

Except as otherwise provided in the Rules, a hole is won by the side which holes its ball in the fewer strokes. In a handicap match the lower net score wins the hole.

2-2. Halved Hole

A hole is halved if each side holes out in the same number of strokes.

When a player has holed out and his opponent has been left with a stroke for the half, if the player thereafter incurs a penalty, the hole is halved.

2-3. Reckoning of Holes

The reckoning of holes is kept by the terms: so many "holes up" or "all square," and so many "to play."

A side is "dormie" when it is as many holes up as there are holes remaining to be played.

2-4. Winner of Match

A match (which consists of a stipulated round, unless otherwise decreed by the Committee) is won by the side which is leading by a number of holes greater than the number of holes remaining to be played.

A side may concede a match at any time prior to the conclusion of the match.

The Committee may, for the purpose of settling a tie, extend the stipulated round to as many holes as are required for a match to be won.

2-5. Claims

In match play, if a doubt or dispute arises between the players and no duly authorized representative of the Committee is available within a reasonable time, the players shall continue the match without delay. Any claim, if it is to be considered by the Committee, must be made before any player in the match plays from the next teeing ground or, in the case of the last hole of the match, before all players in the match leave the putting green.

No later claim shall be considered unless it is based on facts previously unknown to the player making the claim and the player making the claim had been given wrong information (Rules 6-2a and 9) by an opponent. In any case, no later claim shall be considered after the result of the match has been officially announced, unless the Committee is satisfied that the opponent knew he was giving wrong information.

2-6. General Penalty

The penalty for a breach of a Rule in match play is loss of hole except when otherwise provided.

Rule 3. Stroke Play

3-1. Winner

The competitor who plays the stipulated round or rounds in the fewest strokes is the winner.

3-2. Failure to Hole Out

If a competitor fails to hole out at any hole before he has played a stroke from the next teeing ground or, in the case of the last hole of the round, before he has left the putting green, *he shall be disqualified.*

3-3. Doubt as to Procedure

In stroke play only, when during play of a hole a competitor is doubtful of his rights or procedure, he may, without penalty, play a second ball. After the doubtful situation has arisen and before taking further action, he should announce to his marker his decision to proceed under this Rule and which ball he will score with if the Rules permit.

On completing the round, the competitor shall report the facts immediately to the Committee; if he fails to do so, *he shall be disqualified.* If the Rules allow the procedure selected in advance by the competitor, the score with the ball selected shall be his score for the hole. If the competitor fails to announce in advance his procedure or selection, the ball with the higher score shall count if the Rules allow the procedure adopted for such ball.

Note: A second ball played under Rule 3-3 is not a provisional ball under Rule 27-2.

3-4. Refusal to Comply with a Rule

If a competitor refuses to comply with a Rule affecting

the rights of another competitor, *he shall be disqualified.*

3-5. General Penalty

The penalty for a breach of a Rule in stroke play is two strokes except when otherwise provided.

CLUBS AND THE BALL

The United States Golf Association and the Royal and Ancient Golf Club of St. Andrews reserve the right to change the Rules and make and change the interpretations relating to clubs, balls and other implements at any time.

Rule 4. Clubs

If a manufacturer is in doubt as to whether a club which he proposes to manufacture conforms with Rule 4 and Appendix II, he should submit a sample to the United States Golf Association for a ruling, such sample to become its property for reference purposes.

A player in doubt as to the conformity of a club should consult the United States Golf Association.

4-1. Form and Make of Clubs

A club is an implement designed to be used for striking the ball.

A putter is a club designed primarily for use on the putting green.

The player's clubs shall conform with the provisions of this Rule and with the specifications and interpretations set forth in Appendix II.

a. GENERAL

The club shall be composed of a shaft and a head. All parts of the club shall be fixed so that the club is one unit. The club shall not be designed to be adjustable except for weight. The club shall not be substantially different from the traditional and customary form and make.

b. SHAFT

The shaft shall be generally straight, with the same bending and twisting properties in any direction, and shall be attached to the clubhead at the heel either directly or through a single plain neck or socket. A putter shaft may be attached to any point in the head.

c. GRIP

The grip consists of that part of the shaft designed to be held by the player and any material added to it for the purpose of obtaining a firm hold. The grip shall be substantially straight and plain in form and shall not be molded for any part of the hands.

d. CLUBHEAD

The length of the clubhead, from heel to toe, shall be greater than the breadth from face to back. The clubhead shall be generally plain in shape.

The clubhead shall have only one face designed for striking the ball, except that a putter may have two such faces if the loft of each is substantially the same and does not exceed ten degrees.

e. CLUB FACE

The face shall not have any degree of concavity and, in relation to the ball, shall be hard and rigid. It shall be generally smooth except for such markings as are permitted by Appendix II. If the basic structural material of the head and face of a club, other than a putter, is metal, no inset or attachment is permitted.

f. WEAR

A club which conforms to Rule 4-1 when new is deemed to conform after wear through normal use. Any part of a club which has been purposely altered is regarded as new and must conform, in the altered state, to the Rules.

g. DAMAGE

A club which ceases to conform to Rule 4-1 because of damage sustained in the normal course of play may be used in its damaged state, but only for the remainder of the stipulated round during which such damage was sustained. A club which ceases to conform because of damage sustained other than in the normal course of play shall not be used unless it is repaired so as to conform to Rule 4-1.

4-2. Playing Characteristics Not to Be Changed

During a stipulated round, the playing characteristics of a club shall not be purposely changed, except that damage occurring during such round may be repaired, provided play is not unduly delayed. Damage which occurred prior to the round may be repaired, provided the playing characteristics are not changed.

4-3. Foreign Material

No foreign material shall be applied to the club face for the purpose of influencing the movement of the ball.

PENALTY FOR BREACH OF RULE 4-1, -2 or -3:
Disqualification.

4-4. Maximum of Fourteen Clubs

a. SELECTION AND REPLACEMENT OF CLUBS

The player shall start a stipulated round with not more than fourteen clubs. He is limited to the clubs thus selected for that round except that, without unduly delaying play, he may:

(i) if he started with fewer than fourteen, add as many as will bring his total to that number; and

(ii) replace, with any club, a club which becomes unfit for play in the normal course of play.

The addition or replacement of a club or clubs may not be made by borrowing from any other person playing on the course.

b. PARTNERS MAY SHARE CLUBS

Partners may share clubs, provided that the total number of clubs carried by the partners so sharing does not exceed fourteen.

PENALTY FOR BREACH OF RULE 4-4a or b,
REGARDLESS OF NUMBER OF EXCESS CLUBS CARRIED:

Match play — At the conclusion of the hole at which the breach is discovered, the state of the match shall be adjusted by deducting one hole for each hole at which a breach occurred. Maximum deduction per round: two holes.

Stroke play — Two strokes for each hole at which any breach occurred; maximum penalty per round: four strokes.

Bogey and par competitions — Penalties as in match play.

Stableford competitions — See Rule 32-1b.

c. EXCESS CLUB DECLARED OUT OF PLAY

Any club carried or used in breach of this Rule shall be declared out of play by the player immediately upon discovery that a breach has occurred and thereafter shall not be used by the player during the round *under penalty of disqualification.*

Rule 5. The Ball

5-1. General

The ball the player uses shall conform to specifications set forth in Appendix III on maximum weight, minimum size, spherical symmetry, initial velocity and overall distance when tested under specified conditions.

5-2. Foreign Material Prohibited

No foreign material shall be applied to a ball for the purpose of changing its playing characteristics.

PENALTY FOR BREACH OF RULE 5-1 or 5-2:
Disqualification.

5-3. Ball Unfit for Play

A ball is unfit for play if it is visibly cut or out of shape or so cracked, pierced or otherwise damaged as to interfere with its true flight or true roll or its normal behavior when struck. A ball is not unfit for play solely because mud or other materials adhere to it, its surface is scratched or its paint is damaged or discolored.

If a player has reason to believe his ball has become unfit for play during play of the hole being played, he may during the play of such hole lift his ball without penalty to determine whether it is unfit, provided he announces his intention in advance to his opponent in match play or his marker or a fellow-competitor in stroke play and gives his opponent, marker or fellow-competitor an opportunity to examine the ball. If he lifts the ball without announcing his intention in advance or giving his opponent, marker or fellow-competitor an opportunity to examine the ball, *he shall incur a penalty of one stroke.*

If it is determined that the ball has become unfit for play during play of the hole being played, the player may substitute another ball, placing it on the spot where the original ball lay. Otherwise, the original ball shall be replaced.

If a ball breaks into pieces as a result of a stroke, the stroke shall be replayed without penalty (see Rule 20-5).

*PENALTY FOR BREACH OF RULE 5-3:
Match play — Loss of hole; Stroke play — Two strokes.*

If a player incurs the general penalty for breach of Rule 5-3, no additional penalty under the Rule shall be applied.

Note 1: The ball may not be cleaned to determine whether it is unfit for play — see Rule 21.

Note 2: If the opponent, marker or fellow-competitor wishes to dispute a claim of unfitness, he must do so before the player plays another ball.

PLAYER'S RESPONSIBILITIES
Rule 6. The Player

Definition

A "marker" is one who is appointed by the Committee to record a competitor's score in stroke play. He may be a fellow-competitor. He is not a referee.

A marker should not lift a ball or mark its position unless authorized to do so by the competitor and, unless he is a fellow-competitor, should not attend the flagstick or stand at the hole or mark its position.

6-1. Conditions of Competition

The player is responsible for knowing the conditions under which the competition is to be played (Rule 33-1).

6-2. Handicap

a. MATCH PLAY

Before starting a match in a handicap competition, the player shall declare to his opponent the handicap to which he is entitled under the conditions of the competition. If a player declares and begins the match with a higher handicap which would affect the number of strokes given or received, *he shall be disqualified*; otherwise, the player shall play off the declared handicap.

b. STROKE PLAY

In any round of a handicap competition, the competitor shall ensure that the handicap to which he is entitled under the conditions of the competition is recorded on his score card before it is returned to the Committee. If no handicap is recorded on his score card before it is returned, or if the recorded handicap is higher than that to which he is entitled and this affects the number of strokes received, *he shall be disqualified* from that round of the handicap competition; otherwise, the score shall stand.

Note: It is the player's responsibility to know the holes at which handicap strokes are to be given or received.

6-3. Time of Starting and Groups

a. TIME OF STARTING

The player shall start at the time laid down by the Committee.

b. GROUPS

In stroke play, the competitor shall remain throughout the round in the group arranged by the Committee unless the Committee authorizes or ratifies a change.

PENALTY FOR BREACH OF RULE 6-3: *Disqualification.*

(Best-ball and four-ball play — see Rules 30-3a and 31-2.)

Note: The Committee may provide in the conditions of a competition (Rule 33-1) that, in the absence of circumstances which warrant waiving the penalty of disqualification as provided in Rule 33-7, if the player arrives at his starting point, ready to play, within five minutes of his starting time, the penalty for failure to start on time is *loss of the first hole to be played in match play or two strokes in stroke play* instead of disqualification.

6-4. Caddie

The player may have only one caddie at any one time, *under penalty of disqualification.*

For any breach of a Rule by his caddie, the player incurs the relative penalty.

6-5. Ball

The responsibility for playing the proper ball rests with the player. Each player should put an identification mark on his ball.

6-6. Scoring in Stroke Play

a. RECORDING SCORES

After each hole the marker should check the score with the competitor. On completion of the round the marker shall sign the card and hand it to the competitor; if more than one marker records the scores, each shall sign for the part for which he is responsible.

b. CHECKING SCORES

The competitor shall check his score for each hole, settle any doubtful points with the Committee, ensure that the marker has signed the card, countersign the card himself and return it to the Committee as soon as possible. The competitor is responsible for the correctness of the score recorded for each hole.

PENALTY FOR BREACH OF RULE 6-6b: *Disqualification.*

Note: As to the Committee's responsibility to add the scores and apply the recorded handicap, see Rule 33-5.

c. NO ALTERATION OF SCORES

No alteration may be made on a card after the competitor has returned it to the Committee.

If the competitor returns a score for any hole lower than actually taken, *he shall be disqualified.* If he returns a score for any hole higher than actually taken, the score as returned shall stand.

Note: In four-ball stroke play, see also Rule 31-4 and -7a.

6-7. Undue Delay

The player shall play without undue delay. Between completion of a hole and playing from the next teeing ground, the player shall not unduly delay play.

PENALTY FOR BREACH OF RULE 6-7:
Match play — Loss of hole; Stroke play — Two strokes.
For repeated offense — Disqualification.
If the player unduly delays play between holes, he is delaying the play of the next hole and the penalty applies to that hole.

6-8. Discontinuance of Play

a. WHEN PERMITTED

The player shall not discontinue play unless:

(i) the Committee has suspended play;

(ii) he believes there is danger from lightning;

(iii) he is seeking a decision from the Committee on a doubtful or disputed point (see Rules 2-5 and 34-3); or

(iv) there is some other good reason such as sudden illness.

Bad weather is not of itself a good reason for discontinuing play.

If the player discontinues play without specific permission from the Committee, he shall report to the Committee as soon as practicable. If he does so and the Committee considers his reason satisfactory, the player incurs no penalty. Otherwise, *the player shall be disqualified.*

Exception in match play: Players discontinuing match play by agreement are not subject to disqualification unless by so doing the competition is delayed.

Note: Leaving the course does not of itself constitute discontinuance of play.

b. PROCEDURE

When play is discontinued in accordance with the Rules, it should, if feasible, be discontinued after the completion of the play of a hole. If this is not feasible, the player should lift his ball. The ball may be cleaned when so lifted. If a ball has been so lifted, the player shall,

when play is resumed, place a ball on the spot from which the original ball was lifted.

PENALTY FOR BREACH OF RULE 6-8b:
Match play — Loss of hole; Stroke play — Two strokes.

Rule 7. Practice

7-1. Before or Between Rounds

a. MATCH PLAY

On any day of a match play competition, a player may practice on the competition course before a round.

b. STROKE PLAY

On any day of a stroke competition or play-off, a competitor shall not practice on the competition course or test the surface of any putting green on the course before a round or play-off. When two or more rounds of a stroke competition are to be played over consecutive days, practice between those rounds on any competition course remaining to be played is prohibited.

Exception: Practice putting or chipping on or near the first teeing ground before starting a round or play-off is permitted.

PENALTY FOR BREACH OF RULE 7-1b: *Disqualification.*

Note: The Committee may in the conditions of a competition (Rule 33-1) prohibit practice on the competition course on any day of a match play competition or permit practice on the competition course or part of the course (Rule 33-2c) on any day of or between rounds of a stroke competition.

7-2. During Round

A player shall not play a practice stroke either during the play of a hole or between the play of two holes except that, between the play of two holes, the player may practice putting or chipping on or near the putting green of the hole last played, any practice putting green or the teeing ground of the next hole to be played in the round, provided such practice stroke is not played from a hazard and does not unduly delay play (Rule 6-7).

Exception: When play has been suspended by the Committee, a player may, prior to resumption of play, practice (a) as provided in this Rule, (b) anywhere other than on the competition course and (c) as otherwise permitted by the Committee.

PENALTY FOR BREACH OF RULE 7-2:
Match play — Loss of hole; Stroke play — Two strokes.
In the event of a breach between the play of two holes, the penalty applies to the next hole.

Note 1: A practice swing is not a practice stroke and may be taken at any place, provided the player does not breach the Rules.

Note 2: The Committee may prohibit practice on or near the putting green of the hole last played.

Rule 8. Advice; Indicating Line of Play

Definition

"Advice" is any counsel or suggestion which could influence a player in determining his play, the choice of a club or the method of making a stroke.

Information on the Rules or on matters of public information, such as the position of hazards or the flag-stick on the putting green, is not advice.

8-1. Advice

Except as provided in Rule 8-2, a player may give advice to, or ask for advice from, only his partner or either of their caddies.

Note: In a team competition without concurrent individual competition, the Committee may in the conditions of the competition (Rule 33-1) permit each team to appoint one person, *e.g.,* team captain or coach, who may give advice to members of that team. Such person shall be identified to the Committee prior to the start of the competition.

8-2. Indicating Line of Play

a. OTHER THAN ON PUTTING GREEN

Except on the putting green, a player may have the line

of play indicated to him by anyone, but no one shall stand on or close to the line while the stroke is being played. Any mark placed during the play of a hole by the player or with his knowledge to indicate the line shall be removed before the stroke is played.

Exception: Flagstick attended or held up — Rule 17-1.

b. ON THE PUTTING GREEN

When the player's ball is on the putting green, the player's caddie, his partner or his partner's caddie may, before the stroke is played, point out a line for putting, but in so doing the putting green shall not be touched in front of, to the side of, or behind the hole. No mark shall be placed anywhere on the putting green to indicate a line for putting.

PENALTY FOR BREACH OF RULE:
Match play — Loss of hole; Stroke play — Two strokes.

Rule 9. Information as to Strokes Taken

9-1. General

The number of strokes a player has taken shall include any penalty strokes incurred.

9-2. Match Play

A player who has incurred a penalty shall inform his opponent as soon as practicable. If he fails to do so, he shall be deemed to have given wrong information, even though he was not aware that he had incurred a penalty.

An opponent is entitled to ascertain from the player, during the play of a hole, the number of strokes he has taken and, after play of a hole, the number of strokes taken on the hole just completed.

If during the play of a hole the player gives or is deemed to give wrong information as to the number of strokes taken, he shall incur no penalty if he corrects the mistake before his opponent has played his next stroke. If after play of a hole the player gives or is deemed to give wrong information as to the number of strokes taken on the hole just completed, he shall incur no penalty if he corrects his mistake before any player plays from the next teeing ground or, in the case of the last hole of the match, before all players leave the putting green. If the player fails so to correct the wrong information, *he shall lose the hole.*

9-3. Stroke Play

A competitor who has incurred a penalty should inform his marker as soon as practicable.

ORDER OF PLAY
Rule 10. Order of Play

10-1. Match Play

a. TEEING GROUND

The side entitled to play first from the teeing ground is said to have the "honor."

The side which shall have the honor at the first teeing ground shall be determined by the order of the draw. In the absence of a draw, the honor should be decided by lot.

The side which wins a hole shall take the honor at the next teeing ground. If a hole has been halved, the side which had the honor at the previous teeing ground shall retain it.

b. OTHER THAN ON TEEING GROUND

When the balls are in play, the ball farther from the hole shall be played first. If the balls are equidistant from the hole, the ball to be played first should be decided by lot.

Exception: Rule 30-3c (best-ball and four-ball match play).

c. PLAYING OUT OF TURN

If a player plays when his opponent should have played, the opponent may immediately require the player to abandon the ball so played and, without penalty, play a ball in correct order (see Rule 20-5).

10-2. Stroke Play

a. TEEING GROUND

The competitor entitled to play first from the teeing ground is said to have the "honor."

The competitor who shall have the honor at the first

teeing ground shall be determined by the order of the draw. In the absence of a draw, the honor should be decided by lot.

The competitor with the lowest score at a hole shall take the honor at the next teeing ground. The competitor with the second lowest score shall play next and so on. If two or more competitors have the same score at a hole, they shall play from the next teeing ground in the same order as at the previous teeing ground.

b. OTHER THAN ON TEEING GROUND

When the balls are in play, the ball farthest from the hole shall be played first. If two or more balls are equidistant from the hole, the ball to be played first should be decided by lot.

Exceptions: Rules 22 (ball interfering with or assisting play) and 31-5 (four-ball stroke play).

c. PLAYING OUT OF TURN

If a competitor plays out of turn, no penalty shall be incurred and the ball shall be played as it lies. If, however, the Committee determines that competitors have agreed to play in an order other than that set forth in Clauses 2a and 2b of this Rule to give one of them an advantage, *they shall be disqualified.*

(Incorrect order of play in threesomes and foursomes stroke play — see Rule 29-3.)

10-3. Provisional Ball or Second Ball from Teeing Ground

If a player plays a provisional ball or a second ball from a teeing ground, he should do so after his opponent or fellow-competitor has played his first stroke. If a player plays a provisional ball or a second ball out of turn, Clauses 1c and 2c of this Rule shall apply.

10-4. Ball Moved in Measuring

If a ball is moved in measuring to determine which ball is farther from the hole, no penalty is incurred and the ball shall be replaced.

TEEING GROUND
Rule 11. Teeing Ground

Definition

The "teeing ground" is the starting place for the hole to be played. It is a rectangular area two club-lengths in depth, the front and the sides of which are defined by the outside limits of two tee-markers. A ball is outside the teeing ground when all of it lies outside the teeing ground.

11-1. Teeing

In teeing, the ball may be placed on the ground, on an irregularity of surface created by the player on the ground or on a tee, sand or other substance in order to raise it off the ground.

A player may stand outside the teeing ground to play a ball within it.

When the first stroke with any ball (including a provisional ball) is played from the teeing ground, the tee-markers are immovable obstructions (see Rule 24-2).

11-2. Ball Falling Off Tee

If a ball, when not in play, falls off a tee or is knocked off a tee by the player in addressing it, it may be re-teed without penalty, but if a stroke is made at the ball in these circumstances, whether the ball is moving or not, the stroke shall be counted but no penalty shall be incurred.

11-3. Playing Outside Teeing Ground

a. MATCH PLAY

If a player, when starting a hole, plays a ball from outside the teeing ground, the opponent may immediately require the player to replay the stroke from within the teeing ground, without penalty.

b. STROKE PLAY

If a competitor, when starting a hole, plays a ball from outside the teeing ground, *he shall be penalized two strokes* and shall then play a ball from within the teeing ground. Strokes played by a competitor from outside the teeing ground do not count in his score. If the competitor fails to rectify his mistake before making a stroke on the next teeing ground or, in the case of the last hole of the round, before leaving the putting green, *he shall be disqualified.*

PLAYING THE BALL

Rule 12. Searching for and Identifying Ball
Definitions

A "hazard" is any bunker or water hazard.

A "bunker" is a hazard consisting of a prepared area of ground, often a hollow, from which turf or soil has been removed and replaced with sand or the like. Grass-covered ground bordering or within a bunker is not part of the bunker.

A "water hazard" is any sea, lake, pond, river, ditch, surface drainage ditch or other open water course (whether or not containing water) and anything of a similar nature.

All ground or water within the margin of a water hazard is part of the water hazard. The margin of a water hazard is deemed to extend vertically upwards. Stakes and lines defining the margins of water hazards are in the hazards.

12-1. Searching for Ball; Seeing Ball

If a ball lies in long grass, rushes, bushes, whins, heather or the like, only so much thereof may be touched as will enable the player to find and identify his ball, except that nothing shall be done which improves its lie, the area of his intended swing or his line of play.

A player is not necessarily entitled to see his ball when playing a stroke.

In a hazard, if the ball is covered by loose impediments or sand, the player may remove only as much thereof as will enable him to see a part of the ball. If the ball is moved in such removal, no penalty is incurred and the ball shall be replaced. As to removal of loose impediments outside a hazard, see Rule 23.

If a ball lying in casual water, ground under repair or a hole, cast or runway made by a burrowing animal, a reptile or a bird is accidentally moved during search, no penalty is incurred; the ball shall be replaced, unless the player elects to proceed under Rule 25-1b.

If a ball is believed to be lying in water in a water hazard, the player may probe for it with a club or otherwise. If the ball is moved in so doing, no penalty shall be incurred; the ball shall be replaced, unless the player elects to proceed under Rule 26-1.

PENALTY FOR BREACH OF RULE 12-1:
Match play — Loss of hole; Stroke play — Two strokes.

12-2. Identifying Ball

The responsibility for playing the proper ball rests with the player. Each player should put an identification mark on his ball.

Except in a hazard, the player may, without penalty, lift a ball he believes to be his own for the purpose of identification and clean it to the extent necessary for identification. If the ball is the player's ball, he shall replace it on the spot from which it was lifted. Before the player lifts the ball, he shall announce his intention to his opponent in match play or his marker or a fellow-competitor in stroke play and give his opponent, marker or fellow-competitor an opportunity to observe the lifting and replacement. If he lifts the ball without announcing his intention in advance or giving his opponent, marker or fellow-competitor an opportunity to observe, or if he lifts his ball for identification in a hazard, *he shall incur a penalty of one stroke* and the ball shall be replaced.

If a player who is required to replace a ball fails to do so, *he shall incur the penalty* for a breach of Rule 20-3a, but no additional penalty under Rule 12-2 shall be applied.

Rule 13. Ball Played As It Lies; Lie, Area of Intended Swing and Line of Play; Stance
Definitions

A "hazard" is any bunker or water hazard.

A "bunker" is a hazard consisting of a prepared area of ground, often a hollow, from which turf or soil has been removed and replaced with sand or the like. Grass-covered ground bordering or within a bunker is not part of the bunker.

A "water hazard" is any sea, lake, pond, river, ditch, surface drainage ditch or other open water course (whether or not containing water) and anything of a similar nature.

All ground or water within the margin of a water hazard is part of the water hazard. The margin of a water hazard is deemed to extend vertically upwards. Stakes and lines defining the margins of water hazards are in the hazards.

13-1. Ball Played As It Lies

The ball shall be played as it lies, except as otherwise provided in the Rules.

(Ball at rest moved — Rule 18.)

13-2. Improving Lie, Area of Intended Swing or Line of Play

Except as provided in the Rules, a player shall not improve or allow to be improved:
the position or lie of his ball,
the area of his intended swing or
his line of play
by any of the following actions:
moving, bending or breaking anything growing or fixed (including objects defining out of bounds) or
removing or pressing down sand, loose soil, replaced divots, other cut turf placed in position or other irregularities of surface
except as follows:
as may occur in fairly taking his stance,
in making a stroke or the backward movement of his club for a stroke,
on the teeing ground in creating or eliminating irregularities of surface, or
on the putting green in removing sand and loose soil as provided in Rule 16-1a or in repairing damage as provided in Rule 16-1c.
The club may be grounded only lightly and shall not be pressed on the ground.

Exception: Ball lying in or touching hazard — Rule 13-4.

13-3. Building Stance

A player is entitled to place his feet firmly in taking his stance, but he shall not build a stance.

13-4. Ball Lying in or Touching Hazard

Except as provided in the Rules, before making a stroke at a ball which lies in or touches a hazard (whether a bunker or a water hazard), the player shall not:
  a. Test the condition of the hazard or any similar hazard,
  b. Touch the ground in the hazard or water in the water hazard with a club or otherwise, or
  c. Touch or move a loose impediment lying in or touching the hazard.

Exceptions:

1. At address or in the backward movement for the stroke, the club may touch any obstruction or any grass, bush, tree or other growing thing.

2. The player may place his clubs in a hazard, provided nothing is done which may constitute testing the soil or improving the lie of the ball.

3. The player after playing the stroke, or his caddie at any time without the authority of the player, may smooth sand or soil in the hazard, provided that, if the ball still lies in the hazard, nothing is done which improves the lie of the ball or assists the player in his subsequent play of the hole.

PENALTY FOR BREACH OF RULE:
Match play — Loss of hole; Stroke play — Two strokes.
(Searching for ball — Rule 12-1.)

Rule 14. Striking the Ball
Definition

A "stroke" is the forward movement of the club made with the intention of fairly striking at and moving the ball.

14-1. Ball to Be Fairly Struck At

The ball shall be fairly struck at with the head of the club and must not be pushed, scraped or spooned.

14-2. Assistance

In making a stroke, a player shall not accept physical assistance or protection from the elements.

PENALTY FOR BREACH OF RULE 14-1 OR -2:
Match play — Loss of hole; Stroke play — Two strokes.

14-3. Artificial Devices and Unusual Equipment

Except as provided in the Rules, during a stipulated round the player shall not use any artificial device or unusual equipment:

a. For the purpose of gauging or measuring distance or conditions which might affect his play; or

b. Which might assist him in gripping the club, in making a stroke or in his play, except that plain gloves may be worn, resin, tape or gauze may be applied to the grip (provided such application does not render the grip non-conforming under Rule 4-1c) and a towel or handkerchief may be wrapped around the grip.

PENALTY FOR BREACH OF RULE 14-3: *Disqualification.*

14-4. Striking the Ball More than Once

If a player's club strikes the ball more than once in the course of a stroke, the player shall count the stroke and *add a penalty stroke,* making two strokes in all.

14-5. Playing Moving Ball

A player shall not play while his ball is moving.

Exceptions:
Ball falling off tee — Rule 11-2.
Striking the ball more than once — Rule 14-4.
Ball moving in water — Rule 14-6.

When the ball begins to move only after the player has begun the stroke or the backward movement of his club for the stroke, he shall incur no penalty under this Rule for playing a moving ball, but he is not exempt from any penalty incurred under the following Rules:

Ball at rest moved by player — Rule 18-2a.
Ball at rest moving after address — Rule 18-2b.
Ball at rest moving after loose impediment touched — Rule 18-2c.

14-6. Ball Moving in Water

When a ball is moving in water in a water hazard, the player may, without penalty, make a stroke, but he must not delay making his stroke in order to allow the wind or current to improve the position of the ball. A ball moving in water in a water hazard may be lifted if the player elects to invoke Rule 26.

PENALTY FOR BREACH OF RULE 14-5 or -6:
Match play — Loss of hole; Stroke play — Two strokes.

Rule 15. Playing a Wrong Ball

Definition

A "wrong ball" is any ball other than:

a. The ball in play,

b. A provisional ball or

c. In stroke play, a second ball played under Rule 3-3 or Rule 20-7b.

15-1. General

A player must hole out with the ball played from the teeing ground unless a Rule permits him to substitute another ball.

15-2. Match Play

If a player plays a stroke with a wrong ball except in a hazard, *he shall lose the hole.*

If a player plays any strokes in a hazard with a wrong ball, there is no penalty. Strokes played in a hazard with a wrong ball do not count in the player's score.

If the player and opponent exchange balls during the play of a hole, the first to play the wrong ball other than from a hazard shall lose the hole; when this cannot be determined, the hole shall be played out with the balls exchanged.

15-3. Stroke Play

If a competitor plays a stroke with a wrong ball except in a hazard, *he shall add two penalty strokes to his score* and shall then play the correct ball.

If a competitor plays any strokes in a hazard with a wrong ball, there is no penalty.

Strokes played with a wrong ball do not count in a competitor's score.

If a competitor holes out with a wrong ball, but has not made a stroke on the next teeing ground or, in the case of the last hole of the round, has not left the putting green, he may rectify his mistake by playing the correct ball, subject to the prescribed penalty. *The competitor shall be disqualified* if he does not so rectify his mistake.

Note: For procedure to be followed by owner of wrong ball, see Rule 18-1.

THE PUTTING GREEN
Rule 16. The Putting Green

Definitions

The "putting green" is all ground of the hole being played which is specially prepared for putting or otherwise defined as such by the Committee. A ball is on the putting green when any part of it touches the putting green.

A ball is "holed" when it is at rest within the circumference of the hole and all of it is below the level of the lip of the hole.

16-1. General

a. TOUCHING LINE OF PUTT

The line of putt must not be touched except:

(i) the player may move sand, loose soil and other loose impediments by picking them up or by brushing them aside with his hand or a club without pressing anything down;

(ii) in addressing the ball, the player may place the club in front of the ball without pressing anything down;

(iii) in measuring — Rule 10-4;

(iv) in lifting the ball — Rule 16-1b;

(v) in repairing old hole plugs or ball marks — Rule 16-1c; and

(vi) in removing movable obstructions — Rule 24-1.

(Indicating line for putting on putting green — Rule 8-2b.)

b. LIFTING BALL

A ball on the putting green may be lifted and, if desired, cleaned. A ball so lifted shall be replaced on the spot from which it was lifted.

c. REPAIR OF HOLE PLUGS AND BALL MARKS

The player may repair an old hole plug or damage to the putting green caused by the impact of a ball, whether or not the player's ball lies on the putting green. If the ball is moved in the process of such repair, it shall be replaced, without penalty.

d. TESTING SURFACE

During the play of a hole, a player shall not test the surface of the putting green by rolling a ball or roughening or scraping the surface.

e. STANDING ASTRIDE OR ON LINE OF PUTT

The player shall not make a stroke on the putting green from a stance astride, or with either foot touching, the line of the putt or an extension of that line behind the ball. For the purpose of this Clause only, the line of putt does not extend beyond the hole.

f. POSITION OF CADDIE OR PARTNER

While making the stroke, the player shall not allow his caddie, his partner or his partner's caddie to position himself on or close to an extension of the line of putt behind the ball.

g. OTHER BALL TO BE AT REST

A player shall not play a stroke or touch his ball in play while another ball is in motion after a stroke on the putting green.

h. BALL OVERHANGING HOLE

When any part of the ball overhangs the edge of the hole, the player is allowed enough time to reach the hole without unreasonable delay and an additional 10 seconds to determine whether the ball is at rest. If by then the ball has not fallen into the hole, it is deemed to be at rest.

PENALTY FOR BREACH OF RULE 16-1:
Match play — Loss of hole; Stroke play — Two strokes.

16-2. Conceding Opponent's Next Stroke

When the opponent's ball is at rest or is deemed to be at

rest, the player may concede the opponent to have holed out with his next stroke and the ball may be removed by either side with a club or otherwise.

Rule 17. The Flagstick

17-1. Flagstick Attended, Removed or Held Up

Before and during the stroke, the player may have the flagstick attended, removed or held up to indicate the position of the hole. This may be done only on the authority of the player before he plays his stroke.

If the flagstick is attended or removed by an opponent, a fellow-competitor or the caddie of either with the player's knowledge and no objection is made, the player shall be deemed to have authorized it. If a player or a caddie attends or removes the flagstick or stands near the hole while a stroke is being played, he shall be deemed to attend the flagstick until the ball comes to rest.

If the flagstick is not attended before the stroke is played, it shall not be attended or removed while the ball is in motion.

17-2. Unauthorized Attendance

a. MATCH PLAY

In match play, an opponent or his caddie shall not attend or remove the flagstick without the player's knowledge or authority.

b. STROKE PLAY

In stroke play, if a fellow-competitor or his caddie attends or removes the flagstick without the competitor's knowledge or authority while the competitor is making a stroke or his ball is in motion, *the fellow-competitor shall incur the penalty* for breach of this Rule. In such circumstances, if the competitor's ball strikes the flagstick or the person attending it, the competitor incurs no penalty and the ball shall be played as it lies, except that, if the stroke was played from the putting green, the stroke shall be replayed.

PENALTY FOR BREACH OF RULE 17-1 or -2:
Match play — Loss of hole; Stroke play — Two strokes.

17-3. Ball Striking Flagstick or Attendant

The player's ball shall not strike:
a. The flagstick when attended or removed by the player, his partner or either of their caddies, or by another person with the player's knowledge or authority; or
b. The player's caddie, his partner or his partner's caddie when attending the flagstick, or another person attending the flagstick with the player's knowledge or authority, or equipment carried by any such person; or
c. The flagstick in the hole, unattended, when the ball has been played from the putting green.

PENALTY FOR BREACH OF RULE 17-3:
Match play — Loss of hole; Stroke play — Two strokes, and the ball shall be played as it lies.

17-4. Ball Resting Against Flagstick

If the ball rests against the flagstick when it is in the hole, the player or someone authorized by him may move or remove the flagstick and if the ball falls into the hole, the player shall be deemed to have holed out at his last stroke; otherwise, the ball, if moved, shall be placed on the lip of the hole, without penalty.

BALL MOVED, DEFLECTED OR STOPPED
Rule 18. Ball at Rest Moved

Definitions

A ball is deemed to have "moved" if it leaves its position and comes to rest in any other place.

An "outside agency" is any agency not part of the match or, in stroke play, not part of a competitor's side, and includes a referee, a marker, an observer or a forecaddie. Neither wind nor water is an outside agency.

"Equipment" is anything used, worn or carried by or for the player except any ball he has played and any small object, such as a coin or a tee, when used to mark the position of a ball or the extent of an area in which a ball

is to be dropped. Equipment includes a golf cart, whether or not motorized. If such a cart is shared by more than one player, its status under the Rules is the same as that of a caddie employed by more than one player. See "Caddie."

A player has "addressed the ball" when he has taken his stance and has also grounded his club, except that in a hazard a player has addressed the ball when he has taken his stance.

Taking the "stance" consists in a player placing his feet in position for and preparatory to making a stroke.

18-1. By Outside Agency

If a ball at rest is moved by an outside agency, the player shall incur no penalty and the ball shall be replaced before the player plays another stroke. If the ball moved is not immediately recoverable, another ball may be substituted.

(Player's ball at rest moved by another ball — see Rule 18-5.)

18-2. By Player, Partner, Caddie or Equipment

a. GENERAL

When a player's ball is in play, if:
(i) the player, his partner or either of their caddies lifts or moves it, touches it purposely (except with a club in the act of addressing it) or causes it to move except as permitted by a Rule, or
(ii) equipment of the player or his partner causes the ball to move,
the player shall incur a penalty stroke. The ball shall be replaced unless the movement of the ball occurs after the player has begun his swing and he does not discontinue his swing.

Under the Rules no penalty is incurred if a player accidentally causes his ball to move in the following circumstances:
In measuring to determine which ball farther from hole — Rule 10-4
In searching for covered ball in hazard or for ball in casual water, ground under repair, etc. — Rule 12-1
In the process of repairing hole plug or ball mark — Rule 16-1c
In the process of removing loose impediment on putting green — Rule 18-2c
In the process of lifting ball under a Rule — Rule 20-1
In the process of placing or replacing ball under a Rule — Rule 20-3a
In complying with Rule 22 relating to lifting ball interfering with or assisting play
In removal of movable obstruction — Rule 24-1.

b. BALL MOVING AFTER ADDRESS

If a ball in play moves after the player has addressed it other than as a result of a stroke, he shall be deemed to have moved the ball and *shall incur a penalty stroke*, and the ball shall be played as it lies.

c. BALL MOVING AFTER LOOSE IMPEDIMENT TOUCHED

Through the green, if the ball moves after any loose impediment lying within a club-length of it has been touched by the player, his partner or either of their caddies and before the player has addressed it, the player shall be deemed to have moved the ball and *shall incur a penalty stroke*. The player shall replace the ball unless the movement of the ball occurs after he has begun his swing and he does not discontinue his swing.

On the putting green, if the ball moves in the process of removing any loose impediment, it shall be replaced without penalty.

18-3. By Opponent, Caddie or Equipment in Match Play

a. DURING SEARCH

If, during search for a player's ball, it is moved by an opponent, his caddie or his equipment, no penalty is incurred and the player shall replace the ball.

b. OTHER THAN DURING SEARCH

If, other than during search for a ball, the ball is touched or moved by an opponent, his caddie or his equipment, except as otherwise provided in the Rules, *the opponent shall incur a penalty stroke.* The player shall replace the ball.

(Ball moved in measuring to determine which ball farther from the hole — Rule 10-4.)

(Playing a wrong ball — Rule 15-2.)

(Ball moved in complying with Rule 22 relating to lifting ball interfering with or assisting play.)

18-4. By Fellow-Competitor, Caddie or Equipment in Stroke Play

If a competitor's ball is moved by a fellow-competitor, his caddie or his equipment, no penalty is incurred. The competitor shall replace his ball.

(Playing a wrong ball — Rule 15-3.)

18-5. By Another Ball

If a player's ball at rest is moved by another ball, the player's ball shall be replaced.

*PENALTY FOR BREACH OF RULE:
Match play — Loss of hole; Stroke play — Two strokes.
**If a player who is required to replace a ball fails to do so, he shall incur the general penalty for breach of Rule 18 but no additional penalty under Rule 18 shall be applied.*

Note: If it is impossible to determine the spot on which a ball is to be placed, see Rule 20-3c.

Rule 19. Ball in Motion Deflected or Stopped
Definitions

An "outside agency" is any agency not part of the match or, in stroke play, not part of a competitor's side, and includes a referee, a marker, an observer or a forecaddie. Neither wind nor water is an outside agency.

"Equipment" is anything used, worn or carried by or for the player except any ball he has played and any small object, such as a coin or a tee, when used to mark the position of a ball or the extent of an area in which a ball is to be dropped. Equipment includes a golf cart, whether or not motorized. If such a cart is shared by more than one player, its status under the Rules is the same as that of a caddie employed by more than one player. See "Caddie."

19-1. By Outside Agency

If a ball in motion is accidentally deflected or stopped by any outside agency, it is a rub of the green, no penalty is incurred and the ball shall be played as it lies except:

a. If a ball in motion after a stroke other than on the putting green comes to rest in or on any moving or animate outside agency, the player shall, through the green or in a hazard, drop the ball, or on the putting green place the ball, as near as possible to the spot where the outside agency was when the ball came to rest in or on it, and

b. If a ball in motion after a stroke on the putting green is deflected or stopped by, or comes to rest in or on, any moving or animate outside agency, the stroke shall be cancelled and the ball shall be replaced. If the ball is not immediately recoverable, another ball may be substituted.

(Player's ball deflected or stopped by another ball at rest — see Rule 19-5.)

Note: If the referee or the Committee determines that a ball has been deliberately deflected or stopped by an outside agency, including a fellow-competitor or his caddie, further procedure should be prescribed in equity under Rule 1-4.

19-2. By Player, Partner, Caddie or Equipment
a. MATCH PLAY

If a player's ball is deflected or stopped by himself, his partner or either of their caddies or equipment, *he shall lose the hole.*

b. STROKE PLAY

If a competitor's ball is deflected or stopped by himself, his partner or either of their caddies or equipment, *the competitor shall incur a penalty of two strokes.* The ball shall be played as it lies, except when it comes to rest in or on the competitor's, his partner's or either of their caddies' clothes or equipment, in which case the competitor shall through the green or in a hazard drop the ball, or on the

putting green place the ball, as near as possible to where the article was when the ball came to rest in or on it.

Exception: Dropped ball — see Rule 20-2a.

19-3. By Opponent, Caddie or Equipment in Match Play
a. PURPOSELY

If a player's ball is purposely deflected or stopped by an opponent, his caddie or his equipment, *the opponent shall lose the hole.*

Note: In the case of a serious breach of Rule 19-3a, the Committee may impose a penalty of disqualification.

b. ACCIDENTALLY

If a player's ball is accidentally deflected or stopped by an opponent, his caddie or his equipment, no penalty is incurred. The player may play the ball as it lies or, before another stroke is played by either side, cancel the stroke and replay the stroke (see Rule 20-5). If the ball has come to rest in or on the opponent's or his caddie's clothes or equipment, the player may through the green or in a hazard drop the ball, or on the putting green place the ball, as near as possible to where the article was when the ball came to rest in or on it.

Exception: Ball striking person attending flagstick — Rule 17-3b.

19-4. By Fellow-Competitor, Caddie or Equipment in Stroke Play

See Rule 19-1 regarding ball deflected by outside agency.

19-5. By a Ball at Rest

If a player's ball in motion is deflected or stopped by a ball at rest, the player shall play his ball as it lies. In stroke play, if both balls lay on the putting green prior to the stroke, *the player incurs a penalty of two strokes.* Otherwise, no penalty is incurred.

PENALTY FOR BREACH OF RULE:
Match play — Loss of hole; Stroke play — Two strokes.

RELIEF SITUATIONS AND PROCEDURE
Rule 20. Lifting, Dropping and Placing; Playing from Wrong Place

20-1. Lifting

A ball to be lifted under the Rules may be lifted by the player, his partner or another person authorized by the player. In any such case, the player shall be responsible for any breach of the Rules.

The position of the ball shall be marked before it is lifted under a Rule which requires it to be replaced. If it is not marked, the player *shall incur a penalty of one stroke* and the ball shall be replaced. If it is not replaced, *the player shall incur the general penalty* for breach of this Rule but no additional penalty under Rule 20-1 shall be applied.

If a ball is accidentally moved in the process of lifting it under a Rule, no penalty shall be incurred and the ball shall be replaced.

Note: The position of a lifted ball should be marked, if feasible, by placing a ball-marker or other small object immediately behind the ball. If the ball-marker interferes with the play, stance or stroke of another player, it should be placed one or more clubhead-lengths to one side.

20-2. Dropping and Re-dropping
a. BY WHOM AND HOW

A ball to be dropped under the Rules shall be dropped by the player himself. He shall stand erect, hold the ball at shoulder height and arm's length and drop it. If a ball is dropped by any other person or in any other manner and the error is not corrected as provided in Rule 20-6, *the player shall incur a penalty stroke.*

If the ball touches the player, his partner, either of their caddies or their equipment before or after it strikes the ground, the ball shall be re-dropped, without penalty.

(Taking action to influence position or movement of ball — Rule 1-2.)

b. WHERE TO DROP

When a ball is to be dropped, it shall be dropped as near

as possible to the spot where the ball lay, but not nearer the hole, except when a Rule permits it to be dropped elsewhere. If a ball is to be dropped in a hazard, the ball shall be dropped in and come to rest in that hazard.

c. WHEN TO RE-DROP

A dropped ball shall be re-dropped without penalty if it:

(i) rolls into a hazard;

(ii) rolls out of a hazard;

(iii) rolls onto a putting green;

(iv) rolls out of bounds;

(v) rolls back into the condition from which relief was taken under Rule 24-2 (immovable obstruction) or Rule 25 (abnormal ground conditions and wrong putting green);

(vi) rolls and comes to rest more than two club-lengths from where it first struck the ground; or

(vii) rolls and comes to rest nearer the hole than is permitted by the Rules.

If the ball again rolls into such position, it shall be placed as near as possible to the spot where it first struck the ground when re-dropped.

20-3. Placing and Replacing

a. BY WHOM AND WHERE

A ball to be placed under the Rules shall be placed by the player or his partner. A ball to be replaced shall be replaced by the player, his partner or the person who lifted or moved it on the spot where the ball lay. In any such case, the player shall be responsible for any breach of the Rules.

If a ball is accidentally moved in the process of placing or replacing it under a Rule, no penalty shall be incurred and the ball shall be replaced.

b. LIE OF BALL TO BE PLACED OR REPLACED ALTERED

Except in a bunker, if the original lie of a ball to be placed or replaced has been altered, the ball shall be placed in the nearest lie most similar to that which it originally occupied, not more than one club-length from the original lie and not nearer the hole. In a bunker, the original lie shall be recreated as nearly as possible and the ball shall be placed in that lie.

c. SPOT NOT DETERMINABLE

If it is impossible to determine the spot where the ball is to be placed, the ball shall through the green or in a hazard be dropped, or on the putting green be placed, as near as possible to the place where it lay but not nearer the hole.

d. BALL FAILS TO REMAIN ON SPOT

If a ball when placed fails to remain on the spot on which it was placed, it shall be replaced without penalty. If it still fails to remain on that spot, it shall be placed at the nearest spot not nearer the hole where it can be placed at rest.

PENALTY FOR BREACH OF RULE 20-1, -2 or -3:
Match play — Loss of hole; Stroke play — Two strokes.

20-4. Ball in Play When Dropped or Placed

A ball dropped or placed under a Rule governing the particular case is in play.

20-5. Playing Next Stroke from Where Previous Stroke Played

When, under the Rules, a player elects or is required to play his next stroke from where a previous stroke was played, he shall proceed as follows: If the stroke is to be played from the teeing ground, the ball to be played shall be played from anywhere within the teeing ground and may be teed; if the stroke is to be played from through the green or a hazard, it shall be dropped; if the stroke is to be played on the putting green, it shall be placed.

PENALTY FOR BREACH OF RULE 20-5:
Match play — Loss of hole; Stroke play — Two strokes.

20-6. Lifting Ball Wrongly Dropped or Placed

A ball dropped or placed in a wrong place or otherwise not in accordance with the Rules but not played may be lifted, without penalty, and the player shall then proceed correctly.

In match play, if, before the opponent plays his next stroke, the player fails to inform him that the ball has been lifted, *the player shall lose the hole.*

20-7. Playing from Wrong Place

For a ball played outside teeing ground, see Rule 11-3.

a. MATCH PLAY

If a player plays a stroke with a ball which has been dropped or placed under an applicable Rule but in a wrong place, *he shall lose the hole.*

b. STROKE PLAY

If a competitor plays a stroke with a ball which has been (i) dropped or placed under an applicable Rule but in a wrong place or (ii) moved and not replaced in a case where the Rules require replacement, *he shall incur the penalty prescribed by the relevant Rule* and play out the hole with the ball. If a serious breach of the relevant Rule is involved, *the competitor shall be disqualified,* unless the breach has been rectified as provided in the next paragraph.

If a serious breach may be involved and the competitor has not made a stroke on the next teeing ground or, in the case of the last hole of the round, has not left the putting green, the competitor may rectify any such serious breach by *adding two penalty strokes to his score,* dropping or placing a second ball in accordance with the Rules and playing out the hole. The competitor should play out the hole with both balls. On completion of the round the competitor shall report the facts immediately to the Committee; if he fails to do so, *he shall be disqualified.* The Committee shall determine whether a serious breach of the Rule was involved and, accordingly, whether the score with the second ball shall count.

Note: Penalty strokes incurred by playing the ball ruled not to count and strokes subsequently taken with that ball shall be disregarded.

Rule 21. Cleaning Ball

A ball may be cleaned when lifted as follows:

Upon suspension of play in accordance with Rule 6-8b;

For identification under Rule 12-2, but the ball may be cleaned only to the extent necessary for identification;

On the putting green under Rule 16-1b;

For relief from an obstruction under Rule 24-1b or -2b;

For relief from abnormal ground conditions or wrong putting green under Rules 25-1b, -2 and -3;

For relief from a water hazard under Rule 26;

For relief for an unplayable ball under Rule 28; or

Under a Local Rule permitting cleaning the ball.

If the player cleans his ball during the play of a hole except as permitted under this Rule, *he shall incur a penalty of one stroke* and the ball, if lifted, shall be replaced.

If a player who is required to replace a ball fails to do so, *he shall incur the penalty* for breach of Rule 20-3a, but no additional penalty under Rule 21 shall be applied.

Rule 22. Ball Interfering with or Assisting Play

Any player may:

a. Lift his ball if he considers that it might assist any other player or

b. Have any other ball lifted if he considers that it might interfere with his play or assist the play of any other player,

but this may not be done while another ball is in motion. In stroke play, a player required to lift his ball may play first rather than lift. A ball lifted under this Rule shall be replaced.

If a ball is accidentally moved in complying with this Rule, no penalty is incurred and the ball shall be replaced.

PENALTY FOR BREACH OF RULE:
Match play — Loss of hole; Stroke play — Two strokes.

Rule 23. Loose Impediments

Definition

"Loose impediments" are natural objects such as stones, leaves, twigs, branches and the like, dung, worms and insects and casts or heaps made by them, provided they are not fixed or growing, are not solidly embedded and do not adhere to the ball.

Sand and loose soil are loose impediments on the putting green but not elsewhere.

Snow and ice are either casual water or loose impediments, at the option of the player.

Dew is not a loose impediment.

23-1. Relief

Except when both the loose impediment and the ball lie in or touch a hazard, any loose impediment may be removed without penalty. If the ball moves, see Rule 18-2c.

When a player's ball is in motion, a loose impediment on his line of play shall not be removed.

PENALTY FOR BREACH OF RULE:
Match play — Loss of hole; Stroke play — Two strokes.

(Searching for ball in hazard — Rule 12-1.)
(Touching line of putt — Rule 16-1a.)

Rule 24. Obstructions

Definition

An "obstruction" is anything artificial, including the artificial surfaces and sides of roads and paths, except:

a. Objects defining out of bounds, such as walls, fences, stakes and railings;

b. Any part of an immovable artificial object which is out of bounds; and

c. Any construction declared by the Committee to be an integral part of the course.

24-1. Movable Obstruction

A player may obtain relief from a movable obstruction as follows:

a. If the ball does not lie in or on the obstruction, the obstruction may be removed; if the ball moves, no penalty is incurred and the ball shall be replaced.

b. If the ball lies in or on the obstruction, the ball may be lifted, without penalty, and the obstruction removed. The ball shall through the green or in a hazard be dropped, or on the putting green be placed, as near as possible to the spot directly under the place where the ball lay in or on the obstruction, but not nearer the hole. The ball may be cleaned when lifted for relief under Rule 24-1b.

When a ball is in motion, an obstruction on the player's line of play other than an attended flagstick and equipment of the players shall not be removed.

24-2. Immovable Obstruction

a. INTERFERENCE

Interference by an immovable obstruction occurs when a ball lies in or on the obstruction, or so close to the obstruction that the obstruction interferes with the player's stance or the area of his intended swing. If the player's ball lies on the putting green, interference also occurs if an immovable obstruction on the putting green intervenes on his line of putt. Otherwise, intervention on the line of play is not, of itself, interference under this Rule.

b. RELIEF

Except when the ball lies in or touches a water hazard or a lateral water hazard, a player may obtain relief from interference by an immovable obstruction, without penalty, as follows:

(i) *Through the Green:* If the ball lies through the green, the point on the course nearest to where the ball lies shall be determined (without crossing over, through or under the obstruction) which (a) is not nearer the hole, (b) avoids interference (as defined) and (c) is not in a hazard or on a putting green. The player shall lift the ball and drop it within one club-length of the point thus determined on ground which fulfils (a), (b) and (c) above.

Note: The prohibition against crossing over, through or under the obstruction does not apply to the artificial surfaces and sides of roads and paths or when the ball lies in or on the obstruction.

(ii) *In a Bunker:* If the ball lies in or touches a bunker, the player shall lift and drop the ball in accordance with Clause (i) above, except that the ball must be dropped in the bunker.

(iii) *On the Putting Green:* If the ball lies on the putting green, the player shall lift the ball and place it in the nearest position to where it lay which affords relief from interference, but not nearer the hole nor in a hazard.

The ball may be cleaned when lifted for relief under Rule 24-2b.

(Ball rolling back into condition from which relief taken — see Rule 20-2c(v).)

Exception: A player may not obtain relief under Rule 24-2b if (a) it is clearly unreasonable for him to play a stroke because of interference by anything other than an immovable obstruction or (b) interference by an immovable obstruction would occur only through use of an unnecessarily abnormal stance, swing or direction of play.

Note: If a ball lies in or touches a water hazard (including a lateral water hazard), the player is not entitled to relief without penalty from interference by an immovable obstruction. The player shall play the ball as it lies or proceed under Rule 26-1.

PENALTY FOR BREACH OF RULE:
Match play — Loss of hole; Stroke play — Two strokes.

Rule 25. Abnormal Ground Conditions and Wrong Putting Green

Definitions

"Casual water" is any temporary accumulation of water on the course which is visible before or after the player takes his stance and is not in a water hazard. Snow and ice are either casual water or loose impediments, at the option of the player. Dew is not casual water.

"Ground under repair" is any portion of the course so marked by order of the Committee or so declared by its authorized representative. It includes material piled for removal and a hole made by a greenkeeper, even if not so marked. Stakes and lines defining ground under repair are in such ground.

Note 1: Grass cuttings and other material left on the course which have been abandoned and are not intended to be removed are not ground under repair unless so marked.

Note 2: The Committee may make a Local Rule prohibiting play from ground under repair.

25-1. Casual Water, Ground Under Repair and Certain Damage to Course

a. INTERFERENCE

Interference by casual water, ground under repair or a hole, cast or runway made by a burrowing animal, a reptile or a bird occurs when a ball lies in or touches any of these conditions or when the condition interferes with the player's stance or the area of his intended swing.

If the player's ball lies on the putting green, interference also occurs if such condition on the putting green intervenes on his line of putt.

If interference exists, the player may either play the ball as it lies (unless prohibited by Local Rule) or take relief as provided in Clause b.

b. RELIEF

If the player elects to take relief, he shall proceed as follows:

(i) *Through the Green:* If the ball lies through the green, the point on the course nearest to where the ball lies shall be determined which (a) is not nearer the hole, (b) avoids interference by the condition, and (c) is not in a hazard or on a putting green. The player shall lift the ball and drop it without penalty within one club-length of the point thus determined on ground which fulfils (a), (b) and (c) above.

(ii) *In a Hazard:* If the ball lies in or touches a hazard, the player shall lift and drop the ball either:

(a) Without penalty, in the hazard, as near as possible to the spot where the ball lay, but not nearer the hole, on ground which affords maximum available relief from the condition;

or

(b) *Under penalty of one stroke*, outside the hazard, keeping the spot where the ball lay directly between himself and the hole.

Exception: If a ball lies in or touches a water hazard (including a lateral water hazard), the player is not entitled to relief without penalty from a hole, cast or runway made by a burrowing animal, a reptile or a bird. The player shall play the ball as it lies or proceed under Rule 26-1.

(iii) *On the Putting Green:* If the ball lies on the putting green, the player shall lift the ball and place it without penalty in the nearest position to where it lay which affords maximum available relief from the condition, but not nearer the hole nor in a hazard.

The ball may be cleaned when lifted under Rule 25-1b.

(Ball rolling back into condition from which relief taken — see Rule 20-2c(v).)

Exception: A player may not obtain relief under Rule 25-1b if (a) it is clearly unreasonable for him to play a stroke because of interference by anything other than a condition covered by Rule 25-1a or (b) interference by such a condition would occur only through use of an unnecessarily abnormal stance, swing or direction of play.

c. Ball Lost Under Condition Covered by Rule 25-1

It is a question of fact whether a ball lost after having been struck toward a condition covered by Rule 25-1 is lost under such condition. In order to treat the ball as lost under such condition, there must be reasonable evidence to that effect. In the absence of such evidence, the ball must be treated as a lost ball and Rule 27 applies.

(i) *Outside a Hazard* — If a ball is lost outside a hazard under a condition covered by Rule 25-1, the player may take relief as follows: the point on the course nearest to where the ball last crossed the margin of the area shall be determined which (a) is not nearer the hole than where the ball last crossed the margin, (b) avoids interference by the condition and (c) is not in a hazard or on a putting green. He shall drop a ball without penalty within one club-length of the point thus determined on ground which fulfils (a), (b) and (c) above.

(ii) *In a Hazard* — If a ball is lost in a hazard under a condition covered by Rule 25-1, the player may drop a ball either:

(a) Without penalty, in the hazard, as near as possible to the point at which the ball last crossed the margin of the area, but not nearer the hole, on ground which affords maximum available relief from the condition

or

(b) *Under penalty of one stroke*, outside the hazard, keeping the spot at which the ball last crossed the margin of the hazard directly between himself and the hole.

Exception: If a ball lies in a water hazard (including a lateral water hazard), the player is not entitled to relief without penalty for a ball lost in a hole, cast or runway made by a burrowing animal, a reptile or a bird. The player shall proceed under Rule 26-1.

25-2. Embedded Ball

A ball embedded in its own pitch-mark in any closely mown area through the green may be lifted, cleaned and dropped, without penalty, as near as possible to the spot where it lay but not nearer the hole. "Closely mown area"

means any area of the course, including paths through the rough, cut to fairway height or less.

25-3. Wrong Putting Green

If a ball lies on a putting green other than that of the hole being played, the point on the course nearest to where the ball lies shall be determined which (a) is not nearer the hole and (b) is not in a hazard or on a putting green. The player shall lift the ball and drop it without penalty within one club-length of the point thus determined on ground which fulfils (a) and (b) above. The ball may be cleaned when so lifted.

Note: Unless otherwise prescribed by the Committee, the term "a putting green other than that of the hole being played" includes a practice putting green or pitching green on the course.

PENALTY FOR BREACH OF RULE:
Match play — Loss of hole; Stroke play — Two strokes.

Rule 26. Water Hazards (Including Lateral Water Hazards)

Definitions

A "water hazard" is any sea, lake, pond, river, ditch, surface drainage ditch or other open water course (whether or not containing water) and anything of a similar nature.

All ground or water within the margin of a water hazard is part of the water hazard. The margin of a water hazard is deemed to extend vertically upwards. Stakes and lines defining the margins of water hazards are in the hazards.

Note: Water hazards (other than lateral water hazards) should be defined by yellow stakes or lines.

A "lateral water hazard" is a water hazard or that part of a water hazard so situated that it is not possible or is deemed by the Committee to be impracticable to drop a ball behind the water hazard and keep the spot at which the ball last crossed the margin of the water hazard between the player and the hole.

That part of a water hazard to be played as a lateral water hazard should be distinctively marked.

Note: Lateral water hazards should be defined by red stakes or lines.

26-1. Ball in Water Hazard

It is a question of fact whether a ball lost after having been struck toward a water hazard is lost inside or outside the hazard. In order to treat the ball as lost in the hazard, there must be reasonable evidence that the ball lodged therein. In the absence of such evidence, the ball must be treated as a lost ball and Rule 27 applies.

If a ball lies in, touches or is lost in a water hazard (whether the ball lies in water or not), the player may *under penalty of one stroke:*

a. Play his next stroke as nearly as possible at the spot from which the original ball was last played or moved by him (see Rule 20-5);

or

b. Drop a ball behind the water hazard, keeping the point at which the original ball last crossed the margin of the water hazard directly between himself and the hole, with no limit to how far behind the water hazard the ball may be dropped;

or

c. *As additional options available only if the ball lies or is lost in a lateral water hazard,* drop a ball outside the water hazard within two club-lengths of (i) the point where the original ball last crossed the margin of the water hazard or (ii) a point on the opposite margin of the water hazard equidistant from the hole. The ball must be dropped and come to rest not nearer the hole than the point where the original ball last crossed the margin of the water hazard.

The ball may be cleaned when lifted under this Rule.

26-2. Ball Played Within Water Hazard

a. Ball Remains in Hazard

If a ball played from within a water hazard has not crossed any margin of the hazard, the player may:

(i) proceed under Rule 26-1; or

(ii) *under penalty of one stroke,* play his next stroke as nearly as possible at the spot from which the last stroke from outside the hazard was played (see Rule 20-5).

b. BALL LOST OR UNPLAYABLE OUTSIDE HAZARD
OR OUT OF BOUNDS

If a ball played from within a water hazard is lost or declared unplayable outside the hazard or is out of bounds, the player, after taking a stroke-and-distance penalty under Rule 27-1 or 28a, may:

(i) play a ball as nearly as possible at the spot from which the original ball was last played by him (see Rule 20-5); or

(ii) under the penalty prescribed therein, proceed under Rule 26-1b or, as additional options in the case of a lateral water hazard, under Rule 26-1c, using as the reference point the point where the ball last crossed the margin of the hazard before it came to rest in the hazard; or

(iii) *under penalty of one stroke,* play his next stroke as nearly as possible at the spot from which the last stroke from outside the hazard was played (see Rule 20-5).

PENALTY FOR BREACH OF RULE:
Match play — Loss of hole; Stroke play — Two strokes.

Rule 27. Ball Lost or Out of Bounds; Provisional Ball

If the original ball is lost under a condition covered by Rule 25-1 (casual water, ground under repair and certain damage to the course), the player may proceed under that Rule. If the original ball is lost in a water hazard, the player shall proceed under Rule 26.

Such Rules may not be used unless there is reasonable evidence that the ball is lost under a condition covered by Rule 25-1 or in a water hazard.

Definitions

A ball is "lost" if:

a. It is not found or identified as his by the player within five minutes after the player's side or his or their caddies have begun to search for it; or

b. The player has put another ball into play under the Rules, even though he may not have searched for the original ball; or

c. The player has played any stroke with a provisional ball from the place where the original ball is likely to be or from a point nearer the hole than that place, whereupon the provisional ball becomes the ball in play.

Time spent in playing a wrong ball is not counted in the five-minute period allowed for search.

"Out of bounds" is ground on which play is prohibited.

When out of bounds is defined by reference to stakes or a fence, or as being beyond stakes or a fence, the out of bounds line is determined by the nearest inside points of the stakes or fence posts at ground level excluding angled supports.

When out of bounds is defined by a line on the ground, the line itself is out of bounds.

The out of bounds line is deemed to extend vertically upwards and downwards.

A ball is out of bounds when all of it lies out of bounds.

A player may stand out of bounds to play a ball lying within bounds.

A "provisional ball" is a ball played under Rule 27-2 for a ball which may be lost outside a water hazard or may be out of bounds. It ceases to be a provisional ball when the Rule provides either that the player continue play with it as the ball in play or that it be abandoned.

27-1. Ball Lost or Out of Bounds

If a ball is lost outside a water hazard or is out of bounds, the player shall play a ball, *under penalty of one stroke,* as nearly as possible at the spot from which the original ball was last played or moved by him (see Rule 20-5).

27-2. Provisional Ball

a. PROCEDURE

If a ball may be lost outside a water hazard or may be out of bounds, to save time the player may play another ball provisionally as nearly as possible at the spot from which the original ball was played (see Rule 20-5). The player shall inform his opponent in match play or his marker or a fellow-competitor in stroke play that he intends to play a provisional ball, and he shall play it before he or his partner goes forward to search for the original ball. If he fails to do so and plays another ball, such ball is not a provisional ball and becomes the ball in play *under penalty of stroke and distance* (Rule 27-1); the original ball is deemed to be lost.

b. WHEN PROVISIONAL BALL BECOMES BALL IN PLAY

The player may play a provisional ball until he reaches the place where the original ball is likely to be. If he plays a stroke with the provisional ball from the place where the original ball is likely to be or from a point nearer the hole than that place, the original ball is deemed to be lost and the provisional ball becomes the ball in play *under penalty of stroke and distance* (Rule 27-1).

If the original ball is lost outside a water hazard or is out of bounds, the provisional ball becomes the ball in play, *under penalty of stroke and distance* (Rule 27-1).

c. WHEN PROVISIONAL BALL TO BE ABANDONED

If the original ball is neither lost outside a water hazard nor out of bounds, the player shall abandon the provisional ball and continue play with the original ball. If he fails to do so, any further strokes played with the provisional ball shall constitute playing a wrong ball and the provisions of Rule 15 shall apply.

Note: If the original ball lies in a water hazard, the player shall play the ball as it lies or proceed under Rule 26. If it is lost in a water hazard or unplayable, the player shall proceed under Rule 26 or 28, whichever is applicable.

PENALTY FOR BREACH OF RULE:
Match play — Loss of hole; Stroke play — Two strokes.

Rule 28. Ball Unplayable

At any place on the course except in a water hazard a player may declare his ball unplayable. The player is the sole judge as to whether his ball is unplayable.

If the player deems his ball to be unplayable, he shall, *under penalty of one stroke:*

a. Play his next stroke as nearly as possible at the spot from which the original ball was last played or moved by him (see Rule 20-5);

or

b. Drop a ball within two club-lengths of the spot where the ball lay, but not nearer the hole;

or

c. Drop a ball behind the spot where the ball lay, keeping that spot directly between himself and the hole, with no limit to how far behind that spot the ball may be dropped.

If the unplayable ball lies in a bunker and the player elects to proceed under Clause b or c, a ball must be dropped in the bunker.

The ball may be cleaned when lifted under this Rule.

PENALTY FOR BREACH OF RULE:
Match play — Loss of hole; Stroke play — Two strokes.

OTHER FORMS OF PLAY

Rule 29. Threesomes and Foursomes

Definitions

Threesome: A match in which one plays against two, and each side plays one ball.

Foursome: A match in which two play against two, and each side plays one ball.

29-1. General

In a threesome or a foursome, during any stipulated round the partners shall play alternately from the teeing grounds and alternately during the play of each hole. Penalty strokes do not affect the order of play.

29-2. Match Play

If a player plays when his partner should have played, *his side shall lose the hole.*

29-3. Stroke Play

If the partners play a stroke or strokes in incorrect order, such stroke or strokes shall be cancelled and *the side shall be penalized two strokes.* A ball shall then be put in play as nearly as possible at the spot from which the side first played in incorrect order (see Rule 20-5) before a stroke has been played from the next teeing ground or, in the case of the last hole of the round, before the side has left the putting green. If this is not done, *the side shall be disqualified.*

Rule 30. Three-Ball, Best-Ball and Four-Ball Match Play

30-1. Rules of Golf Apply

The Rules of Golf, so far as they are not at variance with the following special Rules, shall apply to three-ball, best-ball and four-ball matches.

30-2. Three-Ball Match Play

In a three-ball match, each player is playing two distinct matches.

a. BALL AT REST MOVED BY AN OPPONENT

Except as otherwise provided in the Rules, if the player's ball is touched or moved by an opponent, his caddie or equipment other than during search, Rule 18-3b applies. *That opponent shall incur a penalty stroke in his match with the player,* but not in his match with the other opponent.

b. BALL DEFLECTED OR STOPPED BY AN OPPONENT ACCIDENTALLY

If a player's ball is accidentally deflected or stopped by an opponent, his caddie or equipment, no penalty shall be incurred. In his match with that opponent the player may play the ball as it lies or, before another stroke is played by either side, he may cancel the stroke and replay the stroke (see Rule 20-5). In his match with the other opponent, the occurrence shall be treated as a rub of the green and the hole shall be played out with the original ball.

Exception: Ball striking person attending flagstick — Rule 17-3b.

(Ball purposely deflected or stopped by opponent — Rule 19-3a.)

30-3. Best-Ball and Four-Ball Match Play

a. REPRESENTATION OF SIDE

A side may be represented by one partner for all or any part of a match; all partners need not be present. An absent partner may join a match between holes, but not during play of a hole.

b. MAXIMUM OF FOURTEEN CLUBS

The side shall be penalized for a breach of Rule 4-4 by any partner.

c. ORDER OF PLAY

Balls belonging to the same side may be played in the order the side considers best.

d. WRONG BALL

If a player plays a stroke with a wrong ball except in a hazard, *he shall be disqualified for that hole,* but his partner incurs no penalty even if the wrong ball belongs to him. The owner of the ball shall replace it on the spot from which it was played, without penalty. If the ball is not immediately recoverable, another ball may be substituted.

e. DISQUALIFICATION OF SIDE

(i) *A side shall be disqualified* for a breach of any of the following by any partner:
Rule 1-3 — Agreement to Waive Rules.
Rule 4-1, -2 or -3 — Clubs.
Rule 5 — The Ball.
Rule 6-2a — Handicap (playing off higher handicap).

Rule 6-4 — Caddie.
Rule 6-7 — Undue Delay (repeated offense).
Rule 14-3 — Artificial Devices and Unusual Equipment.

(ii) *A side shall be disqualified* for a breach of any of the following by all partners:
Rule 6-3 — Time of Starting and Groups.
Rule 6-8 — Discontinuance of Play.

f. EFFECT OF OTHER PENALTIES

If a player's breach of a Rule assists his partner's play or adversely affects an opponent's play, *the partner incurs the relative penalty in addition to any penalty incurred by the player.*

In all other cases where a player incurs a penalty for breach of a Rule, the penalty shall not apply to his partner. Where the penalty is stated to be loss of hole, the effect shall be to disqualify the player for that hole.

g. ANOTHER FORM OF MATCH PLAYED CONCURRENTLY

In a best-ball or four-ball match when another form of match is played concurrently, the above special Rules shall apply.

Rule 31. Four-Ball Stroke Play

In four-ball stroke play two competitors play as partners, each playing his own ball. The lower score of the partners is the score for the hole. If one partner fails to complete the play of a hole, there is no penalty.

31-1. Rules of Golf Apply

The Rules of Golf, so far as they are not at variance with the following special Rules, shall apply to four-ball stroke play.

31-2. Representation of Side

A side may be represented by either partner for all or any part of a stipulated round; both partners need not be present. An absent competitor may join his partner between holes, but not during play of a hole.

31-3. Maximum of Fourteen Clubs

The side shall be penalized for a breach of Rule 4-4 by either partner.

31-4. Scoring

The marker is required to record for each hole only the gross score of whichever partner's score is to count. The gross scores to count must be individually identifiable; otherwise *the side shall be disqualified.* Only one of the partners need be responsible for complying with Rule 6-6a and b.

(Wrong score — Rule 31-7a.)

31-5. Order of Play

Balls belonging to the same side may be played in the order the side considers best.

31-6. Wrong Ball

If a competitor plays a stroke with a wrong ball except in a hazard, *he shall add two penalty strokes to his score for the hole* and shall then play the correct ball. His partner incurs no penalty even if the wrong ball belongs to him.

The owner of the ball shall replace it on the spot from which it was played, without penalty. If the ball is not immediately recoverable, another ball may be substituted.

31-7. Disqualification Penalties

a. BREACH BY ONE PARTNER

A side shall be disqualified from the competition for a breach of any of the following by either partner:
Rule 1-3 — Agreement to Waive Rules.
Rule 3-4 — Refusal to Comply with Rule.
Rule 4-1, -2 or -3 — Clubs.
Rule 5 — The Ball.
Rule 6-2b — Handicap (playing off higher handicap; failure to record handicap).
Rule 6-4 — Caddie.
Rule 6-6b — Checking Scores.
Rule 6-6c — No Alteration of Scores, *i.e.,* when the recorded lower score of the partners is lower than actually played. If the recorded lower score of the partners is higher than actually played, it must stand as returned.

Rule 6-7 — Undue Delay (repeated offense).
Rule 7-1 — Practice Before or Between Rounds.
Rule 14-3 — Artificial Devices and Unusual Equipment.
Rule 31-4 — Gross Scores to Count Not Individually Identifiable.

b. BREACH BY BOTH PARTNERS

A side shall be disqualified for a breach of any of the following by both partners:

Rule 6-3 — Time of Starting and Groups.
Rule 6-8 — Discontinuance of Play.

At the same hole, of a Rule or Rules, the penalty for which is disqualification either from the competition or for a hole.

c. FOR THE HOLE ONLY

In all other cases where a breach of a Rule would entail disqualification, *the competitor shall be disqualified only for the hole at which the breach occurred.*

31-8. Effect of Other Penalties

If a competitor's breach of a Rule assists his partner's play, *the partner incurs the relative penalty in addition to any penalty incurred by the competitor.*

In all other cases where a competitor incurs a penalty for breach of a Rule, the penalty shall not apply to his partner.

Rule 32. Bogey, Par and Stableford Competitions

32-1. Conditions

Bogey, par and Stableford competitions are forms of stroke competition in which play is against a fixed score at each hole. The Rules for stroke play, so far as they are not at variance with the following special Rules, apply.

a. BOGEY AND PAR COMPETITIONS

The reckoning for bogey and par competitions is made as in match play. Any hole for which a competitor makes no return shall be regarded as a loss. The winner is the competitor who is most successful in the aggregate of holes.

The marker is responsible for marking only the gross number of strokes for each hole where the competitor makes a net score equal to or less than the fixed score.

Note: Maximum of 14 clubs — Penalties as in match play — see Rule 4-4.

b. STABLEFORD COMPETITIONS

The reckoning in Stableford competitions is made by points awarded in relation to a fixed score at each hole as follows:

Hole Played In	Points
More than one over fixed score	0
One over fixed score	1
Fixed score	2
One under fixed score	3
Two under fixed score	4
Three under fixed score	5

The winner is the competitor who scores the highest number of points.

The marker shall be responsible for marking only the gross number of strokes at each hole where the competitor's net score earns one or more points.

Note: Maximum of 14 clubs (Rule 4-4) — Penalties applied as follows: From total points scored for the round, deduction of two points for each hole at which any breach occurred; maximum deduction per round: four points.

32-2. Disqualification Penalties

a. FROM THE COMPETITION

A competitor shall be disqualified from the competition for a breach of any of the following:

Rule 1-3 — Agreement to Waive Rules.
Rule 3-4 — Refusal to Comply with Rule.
Rule 4-1, -2 or -3 — Clubs.
Rule 5 — The Ball.
Rule 6-2b — Handicap (playing off higher handicap; failure to record handicap).
Rule 6-3 — Time of Starting and Groups.

Rule 6-4 — Caddie.
Rule 6-6b — Checking Scores.
Rule 6-6c — No alteration of scores, except that the competitor shall not be disqualified when a breach of this Rule does not affect the result of the hole.
Rule 6-7 — Undue Delay (repeated offense).
Rule 6-8 — Discontinuance of Play.
Rule 7-1 — Practice Before or Between Rounds.
Rule 14-3 — Artificial Devices and Unusual Equipment.

b. FOR A HOLE

In all other cases where a breach of a Rule would entail disqualification, *the competitor shall be disqualified only for the hole at which the breach occurred.*

ADMINISTRATION
Rule 33. The Committee

33-1. Conditions

The Committee shall lay down the conditions under which a competition is to be played.

Certain special rules governing stroke play are so substantially different from those governing match play that combining the two forms of play is not practicable and is not permitted. The results of matches played and the scores returned in these circumstances shall not be accepted.

In stroke play the Committee may limit a referee's duties.

33-2. The Course

a. DEFINING BOUNDS AND MARGINS

The Committee shall define accurately:

(i) the course and out of bounds,
(ii) the margins of water hazards and lateral water hazards,
(iii) ground under repair, and
(iv) obstructions and integral parts of the course.

b. NEW HOLES

New holes should be made on the day on which a stroke competition begins and at such other times as the Committee considers necessary, provided all competitors in a single round play with each hole cut in the same position.

Exception: When it is impossible for a damaged hole to be repaired so that it conforms with the Definition, the Committee may make a new hole in a nearby similar position.

c. PRACTICE GROUND

Where there is no practice ground available outside the area of a competition course, the Committee should lay down the area on which players may practice on any day of a competition, if it is practicable to do so. On any day of a stroke competition, the Committee should not normally permit practice on or to a putting green or from a hazard of the competition course.

d. COURSE UNPLAYABLE

If the Committee or its authorized representative considers that for any reason the course is not in a playable condition or that there are circumstances which render the proper playing of the game impossible, it may, in match play or stroke play, order a temporary suspension of play or, in stroke play, declare play null and void and cancel all scores for the round in question. When play has been temporarily suspended, it shall be resumed from where it was discontinued, even though resumption occurs on a subsequent day. When a round is cancelled, all penalties incurred in that round are cancelled.

(Procedure in discontinuing play — Rule 6-8.)

33-3. Times of Starting and Groups

The Committee shall lay down the times of starting and, in stroke play, arrange the groups in which competitors shall play.

When a match play competition is played over an extended period, the Committee shall lay down the limit of time within which each round shall be completed. When players are allowed to arrange the date of their match within these limits, the Committee should announce that the match must be played at a stated time on the last day of the period unless the players agree to a prior date.

33-4. Handicap Stroke Table
The Committee shall publish a table indicating the order of holes at which handicap strokes are to be given or received.

33-5. Score Card
In stroke play, the Committee shall issue for each competitor a score card containing the date and the competitor's name.

The Committee is responsible for the addition of scores and application of the handicap recorded on the card.

In four-ball stroke play, the Committee is responsible for recording the better ball score for each hole, the addition and the application of the handicaps recorded on the card.

33-6. Decision of Ties
The Committee shall announce the manner, day and time for the decision of a halved match or of a tie, whether played on level terms or under handicap.

A halved match shall not be decided by stroke play. A tie in stroke play shall not be decided by a match.

33-7. Modification of Penalty
The Committee has no power to waive a Rule of Golf. A penalty of disqualification, however, may, in exceptional individual cases, be waived or be modified or be imposed if the Committee considers such action warranted.

33-8. Local Rules
a. POLICY

The Committee may make and publish Local Rules for abnormal conditions if they are consistent with the policy of the Governing Authority for the country concerned as set forth in Appendix I to these Rules.

b. WAIVING PENALTY

A penalty imposed by a Rule of Golf shall not be waived by a Local Rule.

Rule 34. Disputes and Decisions

34-1. Claims and Penalties
a. MATCH PLAY

In match play if a claim is lodged with the Committee under Rule 2-5, a decision should be given as soon as possible so that the state of the match may, if necessary, be adjusted.

If a claim is not made within the time limit provided by Rule 2-5, it shall not be considered unless it is based on facts previously unknown to the player making the claim and the player making the claim had been given wrong information (Rules 6-2a and 9) by an opponent. In any case, no later claim shall be considered after the result of the match has been officially announced, unless the Committee is satisfied that the opponent knew he was giving wrong information.

b. STROKE PLAY

No penalty shall be imposed after the competition is closed unless the Committee is satisfied that the competitor has knowingly returned a score for any hole lower than actually taken (Rule 6-6c); no penalty shall be rescinded after the competition is closed. A competition is deemed to have closed when the result of the competition is officially announced or, in stroke play qualifying followed by match play, when the player has teed off in his first match.

34-2. Referee's Decision
If a referee has been appointed by the Committee, his decision shall be final.

34-3. Committee's Decision
In the absence of a referee, the players shall refer any dispute to the Committee, whose decision shall be final.

If the Committee cannot come to a decision, it shall refer the dispute to the Rules of Golf Committee of the United States Golf Association, whose decision shall be final.

If the point in doubt or dispute has not been referred to the Rules of Golf Committee, the player or players have the right to refer an agreed statement through the Secretary of the Club to the Rules of Golf Committee for an opinion as to the correctness of the decision given. The reply will be sent to the Secretary of the Club or Clubs concerned.

If play is conducted other than in accordance with the Rules of Golf, the Rules of Golf Committee will not give a decision on any question.

Appendix I
LOCAL RULES

Rule 33-8 provides:

"The Committee may make and publish Local Rules for abnormal conditions if they are consistent with the policy of the Governing Authority for the country concerned as set forth in Appendix I to these Rules.

"A penalty imposed by a Rule of Golf shall not be waived by a Local Rule."

Among the matters for which Local Rules may be advisable are the following:

1. Obstructions
Clarifying the status of objects which may be obstructions (Rule 24).

Declaring any construction to be an integral part of the course and, accordingly, not an obstruction, *e.g.*, built-up sides and surfaces of teeing grounds, putting greens and bunkers (Rules 24 and 33-2a).

2. Roads and Paths
Providing relief of the type afforded under Rule 24-2b from roads and paths not having artificial surfaces and sides if they could unfairly affect play.

3. Preservation of Course
Preservation of the course by defining areas, including turf nurseries and other parts of the course under cultivation, as ground under repair from which play is prohibited.

4. Unusual Damage to the Course
(other than as covered in Rule 25)

5. Water Hazards
Lateral Water Hazards. Clarifying the status of sections of water hazards which may be lateral water hazards (Rule 26).

Provisional Ball. Permitting play of a provisional ball for a ball which may be in a water hazard of such character that it would be impracticable to determine whether the ball is in the hazard or to do so would unduly delay play. In such case, if a provisional ball is played and the original ball is in a water hazard, the player may play the original ball as it lies or continue the provisional ball in play, but he may not proceed under Rule 26-1.

6. Defining Bounds and Margins
Specifying means used to define out of bounds, hazards, water hazards, lateral water hazards and ground under repair.

7. Ball Drops
Establishment of special areas on which balls may be dropped when it is not feasible to proceed exactly in conformity with Rule 24-2b (immovable obstructions), Rule 26-1 (water hazards and lateral water hazards) and Rule 28 (ball unplayable).

8. Temporary Conditions — Mud, Extreme Wetness
Temporary conditions which might interfere with proper playing of the game, including mud and extreme wetness warranting lifting an embedded ball anywhere through the green (see detailed recommendation below) or removal of mud from a ball through the green.

Lifting an Embedded Ball

Rule 25-2 provides relief without penalty for a ball embedded in its own pitch-mark in any closely mown area through the green.

On the putting green, a ball may be lifted and damage caused by the impact of a ball may be repaired (Rules 16-1b and c).

When permission to lift an embedded ball anywhere through the green would be warranted, the following Local Rule is suggested:

Anywhere "through the green," a ball which is embedded in its own pitch-mark in ground other than sand may be lifted without penalty, cleaned and dropped as near as possible to the spot where it lay but not nearer the hole. (See Rule 20.)

("Through the green" is the whole area of the course except:

a. Teeing ground and putting green of the hole being played;

b. All hazards on the course.)

Practice at Putting Green of Hole Played

When it is desired to prohibit practice on or near a putting green of a hole already played, the following Local Rule is recommended:

A player during a round shall not play any practice stroke on or near the putting green of any hole he has played in the round. (For other practice, see Rules 7 and 33-2c.)

PENALTY FOR BREACH OF LOCAL RULE:
Match play — Loss of hole; Stroke play — Two strokes.

Marking Position of Lifted Ball

When it is desired to require a specific means of marking the position of a lifted ball on the putting green, the following Local Rule is recommended:

Before a ball on the putting green is lifted, its position shall be marked by placing an object, such as a small coin, immediately behind the ball; if the object interferes with another player, it should be moved one or more putterhead-lengths to one side. If the player fails so to mark the position of the ball, *the player shall incur a penalty of one stroke* and the ball shall be replaced. (This modifies Rule 20-1.)

PENALTY FOR BREACH OF LOCAL RULE:
Match play — Loss of hole; Stroke play — Two strokes.

Prohibition Against
Touching Line of Putt with Club

When it is desired to prohibit touching the line of putt with a club in moving loose impediments, the following Local Rule is recommended:

The line of putt shall not be touched with a club for any purpose except to repair old hole plugs or ball marks or during address. (This modifies Rule 16-1a.)

PENALTY FOR BREACH OF LOCAL RULE:
Match play — Loss of hole; Stroke play — Two strokes.

Temporary Obstructions

When temporary obstructions are installed for a competition, the following Local Rule is recommended:

1. Definition

Temporary immovable obstructions include tents, scoreboards, grandstands, refreshment stands, lavatories and, provided it is not mobile or otherwise readily movable, any piece of equipment for photography, press, radio, television and scoring services.

Excluded are temporary power lines and cables (from which relief is provided in Clause 4) and mobile or otherwise readily movable equipment for photography, press, etc. (from which relief is obtainable under Rule 24-1).

2. Interference

Interference by a temporary immovable obstruction occurs when (a) the ball lies in or on the obstruction or so close to the obstruction that the obstruction interferes with the player's stance or the area of his intended swing or (b) the obstruction intervenes between the player's ball and the hole or the ball lies within one club-length of a spot where such intervention would exist.

3. Relief

A player may obtain relief from interference by a temporary immovable obstruction as follows:

a. THROUGH THE GREEN

Through the green, the point on the course nearest to where the ball lies shall be determined which (a) is not nearer the hole, (b) avoids interference as defined in Clause 2 of this Local Rule and (c) is not in a hazard or on a putting green. He shall lift the ball and drop it without penalty within one club-length of the point thus determined on ground which fulfils (a), (b) and (c) above. The ball may be cleaned when so lifted.

b. IN A HAZARD

If the ball lies in a hazard, the player shall lift and drop the ball either:

(i) in the hazard, without penalty, on the nearest ground affording complete relief within the limits specified in Clause 3a above or, if complete relief is impossible, on ground within the hazard affording maximum relief, or

(ii) outside the hazard, *under penalty of one stroke*, as follows: The player shall determine the point on the course nearest to where the ball lies which (a) is not nearer the hole, (b) avoids interference as defined in Clause 2 of this Local Rule and (c) is not in a hazard.) He shall drop the ball within one club-length of the point thus determined on ground which fulfils (a), (b) and (c) above.

The ball may be cleaned when so lifted.

Exception: A player may not obtain relief under Clause 3a or 3b if (a) it is clearly unreasonable for him to play a stroke, or in the case of intervention to play a stroke toward the hole, because of interference by anything other than a temporary immovable obstruction or (b) interference by a temporary immovable obstruction would occur only through use of an unnecessarily abnormal stance, swing or direction of play.

4. Temporary Power Lines and Cables

The above Clauses do not apply to temporary power lines and cables. If such lines and cables are readily movable, the player may obtain relief under Rule 24-1. If they are not readily movable, the player may obtain relief under Rule 24-2b.

If a ball strikes an elevated power line or cable, it must be replaced and replayed, without penalty. If the ball is not immediately recoverable, another ball may be substituted.

Exception: Ball striking elevated junction section of cable rising from the ground shall not be replayed.

5. Re-Dropping

If a dropped ball rolls into a position covered by this Local Rule, or nearer the hole than its original position, it shall be re-dropped without penalty. If it again rolls into such a position, it shall be placed where it first struck the ground when re-dropped.

PENALTY FOR BREACH OF LOCAL RULE:
Match play — Loss of hole; Stroke play — Two strokes.

"Preferred Lies" and "Winter Rules"

The USGA does not endorse "preferred lies" and "winter rules" and recommends that the Rules of Golf be observed uniformly. Ground under repair is provided for in Rule 25. Occasional abnormal conditions which might interfere with fair play and are not widespread should be defined accurately as ground under repair.

However, adverse conditions are sometimes so general throughout a course that the Committee believes "preferred lies" or "winter rules" would promote fair play or help protect the course. Heavy snows, spring thaws, prolonged rains or extreme heat can make fairways unsatisfactory and sometimes prevent use of heavy mowing equipment.

When a Committee adopts a Local Rule for "preferred lies" or "winter rules," it should be in detail and should be interpreted by the Committee, as there is no established code for "winter rules." Without a detailed Local Rule, it is meaningless for a Committee to post a notice merely saying "Winter Rules Today."

The following Local Rule would seem appropriate for the conditions in question, but the USGA will not interpret it:

A ball lying on a "fairway" may be lifted and cleaned, without penalty, and placed within six inches of where it originally lay, not nearer the hole, and so as to preserve as nearly as possible the stance required to play from the original lie. After the ball has been so placed, it is in play, and if it moves after the player has addressed it, *the penalty shall be one stroke* — see Rule 18-2b.

If the adverse conditions extend onto the putting green, the above Local Rule may be altered by adding the words "or the putting green" after the word "fairway."

The above Local Rule does not require a player to move his ball if he does not want to do so. If it is desired to *protect* the course, the above Local Rule should be reworded to make it mandatory rather than permissive to move the ball from certain areas.

Before a Committee adopts a Local Rule permitting "preferred lies" or "winter rules," the following facts should be considered:

1. Such a Local Rule conflicts with the Rules of Golf and the fundamental principle of playing the ball as it lies.

2. "Winter rules" are sometimes adopted under the guise of protecting the course when, in fact, the practical effect is just the opposite — they permit moving the ball to the best turf, from which divots are then taken to injure the course further.

3. "Preferred lies" or "winter rules" tend generally to lower scores and handicaps, thus penalizing the players in competition with players whose scores for handicaps are made under the Rules of Golf.

4. Extended use or indiscriminate use of "preferred lies" or "winter rules" will place players at a disadvantage when competing at a course where the ball must be played as it lies.

Handicapping and "Preferred Lies"

Scores made under a Local Rule for "preferred lies" or "winter rules" may be accepted for handicapping if the Committee considers that conditions warrant.

When such a Local Rule is adopted, the Committee should ensure that the course's normal scoring difficulty is maintained as nearly as possible through adjustment of tee-markers and related methods. However, if extreme conditions cause extended use of "preferred lies" or "winter rules" and the course management cannot adjust scoring difficulty properly, the club should obtain a Temporary Course Rating from its district golf association.

Appendices II and III

Any design in a club or ball which is not covered by Rules 4 and 5 and Appendices II and III, or which might significantly change the nature of the game, will be ruled on by the United States Golf Association and the Royal and Ancient Golf Club of St. Andrews.

Note: Equipment approved for use or marketed prior to January 1, 1984 which conformed to the Rules in effect in 1983 but does not conform to the 1984 Rules may be used until December 31, 1989; thereafter all equipment must conform to the current Rules.

Appendix II
DESIGN OF CLUBS

Rule 4-1 prescribes general regulations for the design of clubs. The following paragraphs provide some detailed specifications and clarify how Rule 4-1 is interpreted.

4-1b. Shaft
GENERALLY STRAIGHT

The shaft must be straight from the top of the grip to a point not more than 5 inches (127mm) above the sole, measured along the axis of the shaft and the neck or socket.

BENDING AND TWISTING PROPERTIES

The shaft must be so designed and manufactured that at any point along its length:

(i) it bends in such a way that the deflection is the same regardless of how the shaft is rotated about its longitudinal axis; and

(ii) it twists the same amount in both directions.

ATTACHMENT TO CLUBHEAD

The neck or socket must not be more than 5 inches (127mm) in length, measured from the top of the neck or socket to the sole along its axis. The shaft and the neck or socket must remain in line with the heel, or with a point to the right or left of the heel, when the club is viewed in the address position. The distance between the axis of the shaft or the neck or socket and the back of the heel must not exceed 0.625 inches (16mm).

Exception for Putters: The shaft or neck or socket of a putter may be fixed at any point in the head and need not remain in line with the heel. The axis of the shaft from the top to a point not more than 5 inches (127mm) above the sole must diverge from the vertical in the toe-heel plane by at least 10 degrees in relation to the horizontal line determining length of head under Appendix II, Clubhead.

4-1c. Grip
(i) For clubs other than putters, the grip must be generally circular in cross-section, except that a continuous, straight, slightly raised rib may be incorporated along the full length of the grip.

(ii) A putter grip may have a non-circular cross-section, provided the cross-section has no concavity and remains generally similar throughout the length of the grip.

(iii) The grip may be tapered but must not have any bulge or waist.

(iv) The axis of the grip must coincide with the axis of the shaft except for a putter.

4-1d. Clubhead
DIMENSIONS

The length and the breadth of a clubhead are measured on horizontal lines between the vertical projections of the extremities when the clubhead is soled in its normal address position. If the heel extremity is not clearly defined, it is deemed to be 0.625 inches (16mm) above the sole.

PLAIN IN SHAPE

Features such as fins or holes are not permitted, but certain exceptions may be made for putters. Any furrows or runners shall not extend into the face. Windows, holes or transparencies for the purpose of aiding the player in positioning himself are not permitted.

4-1e. Club Face
HARDNESS AND RIGIDITY

The club face must not be designed and manufactured to have the effect at impact of a spring which would unduly influence the movement of the ball.

MARKINGS

Except for specified markings, the surface roughness must not exceed that of decorative sandblasting. Markings must not have sharp edges or raised lips, as determined by a finger test. Markings within the area where impact is intended (the "impact area") are governed by the following:

(i) *Grooves.* A series of straight grooves with diverging sides and a symmetrical cross-section may be used. (See diagram.) The width of grooves must be generally consistent and not exceed 0.035 inches (0.9mm) along their length. The distance between edges of adjacent grooves must not be less than three times the width of a groove, and not less than 0.075 inches (1.9mm). The depth of a groove must not exceed 0.020 inches (0.5mm).

(ii) *Punch Marks.* Punch marks may be used. The area of any such mark must not exceed 0.0044 square inches (2.8 sq. mm). A mark must not be closer to an adjacent mark than 0.168 inches (4.3mm), measured from center to center. The depth of a punch mark must not exceed 0.040 inches (1.0mm). If punch marks are used in combination with grooves, a punch mark may not be closer to a groove than 0.168 inches (4.3mm), measured from center to center.

CLUBS

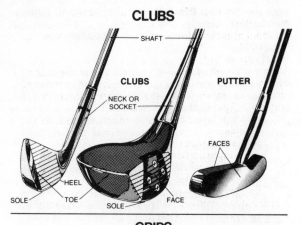

GRIPS

GROOVES

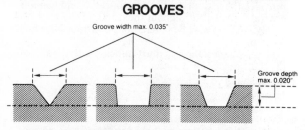

EXAMPLES OF PERMISSIBLE GROOVE CROSS-SECTIONS

DECORATIVE MARKINGS

The center of the impact area may be indicated by a design within the boundary of a square whose sides are 0.375 inches (9.5mm) in length. Such a design must not unduly influence the movement of the ball. Markings outside the impact area must not be greater than 0.040 inches (1.0mm) in depth and width.

NON-METALLIC CLUB FACE MARKINGS

The above specifications for markings do not apply to non-metallic clubs with loft angles less than 24 degrees, but markings which could unduly influence the movement of the ball are prohibited. Non-metallic clubs with a loft or face angle exceeding 24 degrees may have grooves of maximum width 0.040 inches (1.0mm) and maximum depth 1½ times the groove width, but must otherwise conform to the markings specifications above.

Appendix III
THE BALL

a. WEIGHT

The weight of the ball shall not be greater than 1.620 ounces avoirdupois (45.93gm).

b. SIZE

The diameter of the ball shall be not less than 1.680 inches (42.67mm). This specification will be satisfied if, under its own weight, a ball falls through a 1.680 inches diameter ring gauge in fewer than 25 out of 100 randomly selected positions, the test being carried out at a temperature of 23±1°C.

c. SPHERICAL SYMMETRY

The ball shall be designed and manufactured to perform in general as if it were spherically symmetrical.

As outlined in procedures on file at the United States Golf Association, differences in peak angle of trajectory, carry and time of flight will be measured when 40 balls of the same type are launched, spinning 20 about one axis and 20 about another axis.

These tests will be performed using apparatus approved

by the United States Golf Association. If in two successive tests differences in the same two or more measurements are statistically significant at the 5% level of significance and exceed the limits set forth below, the ball type will not conform to the symmetry specification.

MEASUREMENT	MAXIMUM ABSOLUTE DIFFERENCE OF THE MEANS
Peak angle of trajectory	0.9 grid units (approx. 0.4 degrees)
Carry distance	2.5 yards
Flight time	0.16 seconds

Note: Methods of determining whether a ball performs as if it were generally spherically symmetrical may be subject to change as instrumentation becomes available to measure other properties accurately, such as the aerodynamic coefficient of lift, coefficient of drag and moment of inertia.

d. INITIAL VELOCITY

The velocity of the ball shall not be greater than 250 feet (76.2m) per second when measured on apparatus approved by the United States Golf Association. A maximum tolerance of 2% will be allowed. The temperature of the ball when tested shall be 23±1°C.

e. OVERALL DISTANCE STANDARD

A brand of golf ball, when tested on apparatus approved by the USGA on the outdoor range at the USGA Headquarters under the conditions set forth in the Overall Distance Standard for golf balls on file with the USGA, shall not cover an average distance in carry and roll exceeding 280 yards plus a tolerance of 8%. *Note:* The 8% tolerance will be reduced to a minimum of 4% as test techniques are improved.

Exception: In international team competitions, the size of the ball shall not be less than 1.620 inches (41.15 mm) in diameter and the Overall Distance Standard shall not apply.

Note: The Rules of the Royal and Ancient Golf Club of St. Andrews provide for the same specifications as those set forth above except that the size of the ball must not be less than 1.620 inches (41.15 mm) in diameter and there is no Overall Distance Standard.

Appendix IV
MISCELLANEOUS

How to Decide Ties in Handicap Events

Rule 33-6 empowers the Committee to determine how and when a halved match or a stroke play tie shall be decided. The decision should be published in advance.

The USGA recommends:

1. Match Play

A handicap match which ends all square should be played off hole by hole until one side wins a hole. The play-off should start on the hole where the match began. Strokes should be allowed as in the prescribed round.

2. Stroke Play

A handicap stroke competition which ends in a tie should be played off at 18 holes, with handicaps. If a shorter play-off is necessary, the percentage of 18 holes to be played shall be applied to the players' handicaps to determine their play-off handicaps. It is advisable to arrange for a percentage of holes that will result in whole numbers in handicaps; if this is not feasible, handicap stroke fractions of one-half or more shall count as a full stroke, and any lesser fractions shall be disregarded.

Example: In an individual competition, A's handicap is 10 and B's is 8. It would be appropriate to conduct a nine-hole play-off (50% of 18 holes) with A receiving 5 strokes and B 4 strokes.

Pairings for Match Play

General Numerical Draw

For purposes of determining places in the draw, ties in

qualifying rounds other than those for the last qualifying place shall be decided by the order in which scores are returned, the first score to be returned receiving the lowest available number, etc. If it is impossible to determine the order in which scores are returned, ties shall be determined by a blind draw.

Upper Half	Lower Half	Upper Half	Lower Half
64 Qualifiers		32 Qualifiers	
1 vs. 33	2 vs. 34	1 vs. 17	2 vs. 18
17 vs. 49	18 vs. 50	9 vs. 25	10 vs. 26
9 vs. 41	10 vs. 42	5 vs. 21	6 vs. 22
25 vs. 57	26 vs. 58	13 vs. 29	14 vs. 30
5 vs. 37	6 vs. 38	3 vs. 19	4 vs. 20
21 vs. 53	22 vs. 54	11 vs. 27	12 vs. 28
13 vs. 45	14 vs. 46	7 vs. 23	8 vs. 24
29 vs. 61	30 vs. 62	15 vs. 31	16 vs. 32
3 vs. 35	4 vs. 36	16 Qualifiers	
19 vs. 51	20 vs. 52	1 vs. 9	2 vs. 10
11 vs. 43	12 vs. 44	5 vs. 13	6 vs. 14
27 vs. 59	28 vs. 60	3 vs. 11	4 vs. 12
7 vs. 39	8 vs. 40	7 vs. 15	8 vs. 16
23 vs. 55	24 vs. 56	8 Qualifiers	
15 vs. 47	16 vs. 48	1 vs. 5	2 vs. 6
31 vs. 63	32 vs. 64	3 vs. 7	4 vs. 8

Par Computation

"Par" is the score that an expert golfer would be expected to make for a given hole. Par means errorless play without flukes and under ordinary weather conditions, allowing two strokes on the putting green.

Yardages for guidance in computing par are given below. They should not be applied arbitrarily; allowance should be made for the configuration of the ground, any difficult or unusual conditions and the severity of the hazards.

Each hole should be measured horizontally from the middle of the tee area to be used to the center of the green, following the line of play planned by the architect in laying out the hole. Thus, in a hole with a bend, the line at the elbow point should be centered in the fairway in accordance with the architect's intention.

	Yardages for Guidance	
Par	Men	Women
3	up to 250	up to 210
4	251 to 470	211 to 400
5	471 and over	401 to 575
6		576 and over

Handicapping

Par as computed above should not be confused with Course Rating as described in the USGA Golf Handicap System. USGA Handicaps must be based on Course Rating rather than par. See the booklet "Golf Committee Manual and USGA Golf Handicap System."

Flagstick Dimensions

The USGA recommends that the flagstick be at least seven feet in height and that its diameter be not greater than three-quarters of an inch from a point three inches above the ground to the bottom of the hole.

Protection of Persons Against Lightning

As there have been many deaths and injuries from lightning on golf courses, all players, caddies and sponsors of golf are urged to take every precaution for the protection of persons against lightning.

The National Bureau of Standards points out:

"If golf clubs could be impressed with the necessity of calling off matches *before the storm is near enough to be hazardous,* the cases of multiple injury or death among players and spectators could be eliminated."

Raising golf clubs or umbrellas above the head adds to the element of personal hazard during electrical storms.

Metal spikes on golf shoes do little to increase the hazard, according to the Bureau.

Taking Shelter

The following rules for personal safety during thunderstorms are based on material in the Lightning Protection Code, NFPA No. 78-1977; ANSI C5. 1-1975 available

from the National Fire Protection Association, Batterymarch Park, Quincy, Mass. 02269, and the American National Standards Institute, 1430 Broadway, New York, N.Y. 10018:

a. Types of Shelter

Do not go out of doors or remain out during thunderstorms unless it is necessary. Seek shelter inside buildings, vehicles, or other structures or locations which offer protection from lightning, such as:

1. Dwellings or other buildings protected against lightning.
2. Large metal-frame buildings.
3. Large unprotected buildings.
4. Automobiles with metal tops and bodies.
5. Trailers with metal bodies.
6. City streets shielded by nearby buildings.

When it is not possible to choose a location that offers better protection, seek shelter in:

1. Dense woods — avoid isolated trees.
2. Depressed areas — avoid hilltops and high places.
3. Small unprotected buildings, tents and shelters in *low* areas — avoid unprotected buildings and shelters in *high* areas.

b. What to Avoid

Certain locations are extremely hazardous during thunderstorms and should be avoided if at all possible. Approaching thunderstorms should be anticipated and the following locations avoided when storms are in the immediate vicinity:

1. Open fields.
2. Athletic fields.
3. Golf courses.
4. Swimming pools, lakes and seashores.
5. Near wire fences, clotheslines, overhead wires and railroad tracks.
6. Isolated trees.
7. Hilltops and wide open spaces.

In the above locations, it is especially hazardous to be riding in or on any of the following during lightning storms:

1. Tractors and other farm machinery operated on the golf course for maintenance of same.
2. Golf carts, scooters, motorcycles, bicycles.

Discontinuing Play During Lightning

Attention is called to Rules 6-8 and 33-2d.

The USGA especially suggests that players be informed that they have the right to stop play if they think lightning threatens them, even though the Committee may not have specifically authorized it by signal.

The USGA generally uses the following signals and recommends that all local committees do similarly:

Discontinue Play: Three consecutive notes of siren, repeated.

Resume Play: One prolonged note of siren, repeated.

Lightning Protection for Shelters

Shelters on golf courses may best be protected by standard lightning protection systems. Details on the installation of conductors, air terminals and maintenance requirements are included in the Lightning Protection Code. An alternative method of protection of such shelters is through what is known as providing a "cone of protection" with grounded rods or masts and overhead conductors as described in Section 31 of the Lightning Protection Code. Such a system is feasible for small structures, but probably would be more expensive than a standard lightning rod system.

Down conductors should be shielded with non-conductive material, resistant to impact and climatic conditions to a height of approximately 8 feet to protect persons from contact with down conductors. Shelters with earthen floors which are provided with lightning protection systems should have any approved grounding electrodes interconnected by an encircling buried, bare conductor of a type suitable for such service, or such electrodes should be provided with radial conductors run out to a distance of at least 10 feet from the electrode, away from the shelter.

It is recommended that several notices similar to this be

posted at every course. Copies of this notice in poster form may be obtained from the USGA.

Rules of Amateur Status

Any person who considers that any action he is proposing to take might endanger his amateur status should submit particulars to the United States Golf Association for consideration.

Definition of an Amateur Golfer

An amateur golfer is one who plays the game as a non-remunerative or non-profit-making sport.

Rule 1. Forfeiture of Amateur Status at Any Age

The following are examples of acts at any age which violate the Definition of an Amateur Golfer and cause forfeiture of amateur status:

1. Professionalism

a. Receiving payment or compensation for serving as a professional golfer or identifying oneself as a professional golfer.

b. Taking any action for the purpose of becoming a professional golfer.

Note: Such actions include applying for a professional's position; filing application to a school or competition conducted to qualify persons to play as professionals in tournaments; receiving services from or entering into an agreement, written or oral, with a sponsor or professional agent; agreement to accept payment or compensation for allowing one's name or likeness as a skilled golfer to be used for any commercial purpose; and holding or retaining membership in any organization of professional golfers.

2. Playing for Prize Money

Playing for prize money or its equivalent in a match, tournament or exhibition.

Note: A player may participate in an event in which prize money or its equivalent is offered, provided that prior to participation he irrevocably waives his right to accept prize money in that event. (See USGA Policy on Gambling for definition of prize money.)

3. Instruction

Receiving payment or compensation for giving instruction in playing golf, either orally, in writing, by pictures or by other demonstrations, to either individuals or groups.

Exceptions:

1. Golf instruction may be given by an employee of an educational institution or system to students of the institution or system and by camp counselors to those in their charge, provided that the total time devoted to golf instruction during a year comprises less than 50 percent of the time spent during the year in the performance of all duties as such employee or counselor.

2. Payment or compensation may be accepted for instruction in writing, provided one's ability or reputation as a golfer was not a major factor in his employment or in the commission or sale of his work.

4. Prizes, Testimonials and Gifts

a. Acceptance of a prize or testimonial of the following character (this applies to total prizes received for any event or series of events in any one tournament or exhibition, including hole-in-one or other events in which golf skill is a factor):

(i) Of retail value exceeding $350; or

(ii) Of a nature which is the equivalent of money or makes it readily convertible into money.

Exceptions:

1. Prizes of only symbolic value (such as metal trophies).

2. More than one testimonial award may be accepted from different donors even though their total retail value exceeds $350, provided they are not presented so as to evade the $350 value limit for a single award. (Testimonial awards relate to notable performances or contributions to golf, as distinguished from tournament prizes.)

b. Conversion of a prize into money.

c. Accepting expenses in any amount as a prize.

d. Because of golf skill or golf reputation, accepting in connection with any golfing event:

(i) Money, or

(ii) Anything else, other than merchandise of nominal value provided to all players.

5. Lending Name or Likeness

Because of golf skill or golf reputation, receiving or contracting to receive payment, compensation or personal benefit, directly or indirectly, for allowing one's name or likeness as a golfer to be used in any way for the advertisement or sale of anything, whether or not used in or appertaining to golf, except as a golf author or broadcaster as permitted by Rule 1-7.

6. Personal Appearance

Because of golf skill or golf reputation, receiving payment or compensation, directly or indirectly, for a personal appearance, except that reasonable expenses actually incurred may be received if no golf competition or exhibition is involved.

7. Broadcasting and Writing

Because of golf skill or golf reputation, receiving payment or compensation, directly or indirectly, for broadcasting concerning golf, a golf event or golf events, writing golf articles or books, or allowing one's name to be advertised or published as the author of golf articles or books of which he is not actually the author.

Exceptions:

1. Broadcasting or writing as part of one's primary occupation or career, provided instruction in playing golf is not included except as permitted in Rule 1-3.

2. Part-time broadcasting or writing, provided (a) the player is actually the author of the commentary, articles or books, (b) instruction in playing golf is not included except as permitted in Rule 1-3 and (c) the payment or compensation does not have the purpose or effect, directly or indirectly, of financing participation in a golf competition or golf competitions.

8. Golf Equipment

Because of golf skill or golf reputation, accepting golf balls, clubs, golf merchandise, golf clothing or golf shoes, directly or indirectly, from anyone manufacturing such merchandise without payment of current market price.

9. Membership and Privileges

Because of golf skill or golf reputation, accepting membership or privileges in a club or at a golf course without full payment for the class of membership or privileges involved unless such membership or privileges have been awarded (1) as purely and deservedly honorary, (2) in recognition of an outstanding performance or contribution to golf and (3) without a time limit.

10. Expenses

Accepting expenses, in money or otherwise, from any source other than from a member of the player's family or legal guardian to engage in a golf competition or exhibition, or to improve golf skill.

Exceptions: A player may receive a reasonable amount of expenses as follows:

1. JUNIOR COMPETITIONS

As a player in a golf competition or exhibition limited exclusively to players who have not reached their 18th birthday.

2. INTERNATIONAL TEAMS

As a representative of a recognized golf association in an international team match between or among golf associations when such expenses are paid by one or more of the golf associations involved or, subject to the approval of the USGA, as a representative in an international team match conducted by some other athletic organization.

3. USGA PUBLIC LINKS CHAMPIONSHIPS

As a qualified contestant in the USGA Amateur Public Links Championships proper, but only within limits fixed by the USGA.

4. SCHOOL, COLLEGE, MILITARY TEAMS

As a representative of a recognized educational institution or of a military service in (1) team events or (2) other events which are limited to representatives of recognized educational institutions or of military services, respectively. In each case, expenses may be accepted from only an educational or military authority.

5. INDUSTRIAL OR BUSINESS TEAMS

As a representative of an industrial or business golf team in industrial or business golf team competitions, respectively, but only within limits fixed by the USGA. (A statement of such limits may be obtained on request from the USGA.)

6. INVITATION UNRELATED TO GOLF SKILL

As a player invited for reasons unrelated to golf skill, e.g., a celebrity, a business associate or customer, a guest in a club-sponsored competition, etc., to take part in a golfing event.

Note 1: Except as otherwise provided in Exception 6 to Rule 1-10, acceptance of expenses from an employer, a partner or other vocational source is not permissible.

Note 2: Business Expenses — It is permissible to play in a golf competition while on a business trip with expenses paid provided that the golf part of the expenses is borne personally and is not charged to business. Further, the business involved must be actual and substantial, and not merely a subterfuge for legitimizing expenses when the primary purpose is golf competition.

Note 3: Private Transport — Acceptance of private transport furnished or arranged for by a tournament sponsor, directly or indirectly, as an inducement for a player to engage in a golf competition or exhibition shall be considered accepting expenses under Rule 1-10.

11. Scholarships

Because of golf skill or golf reputation, accepting the benefits of a scholarship or grant-in-aid other than in accord with the regulation of the National Collegiate Athletic Association, the Association of Intercollegiate Athletics for Women, or the National Association for Intercollegiate Athletics.

12. Conduct Detrimental to Golf

Any conduct, including activities in connection with golf gambling, which is considered detrimental to the best interests of the game.

Rule 2. Advisory Opinions, Enforcement and Reinstatement

1. Advisory Opinions

Any person who considers that any action he is proposing to take might endanger his amateur status may submit particulars to the staff of the United States Golf Association for advice. If dissatisfied with the staff's advice, he may request that the matter be referred to the Amateur Status and Conduct Committee for decision. If dissatisfied with the Amateur Status and Conduct Committee's decision, he may, by written notice to the staff within 30 days after being notified of the decision, appeal to the Executive Committee, in which case he shall be given reasonable notice of the next meeting of the Executive Committee at which the matter may be heard and shall be entitled to present his case in person or in writing. The decision of the Executive Committee shall be final.

2. Enforcement

Whenever information of a possible violation of the Definition of an Amateur Golfer by a player claiming to be an amateur shall come to the attention of the United States Golf Association, the staff shall notify the player of the possible violation, invite the player to submit such information as the player deems relevant and make such other investigation as seems appropriate under the circumstances. The staff shall submit to the Amateur Status and Conduct Committee all information provided by the player, their findings and their recommendation, and the Amateur Status and Conduct Committee shall decide whether a violation has occurred. If dissatisfied with the Amateur Status and Conduct Committee's decision, the player may, by written notice to the staff within 30 days after being notified of the decision, appeal to the Executive Committee, in which case the player shall be given reasonable notice of the next meeting of the Executive Committee at which the matter may be heard and shall be entitled to present his case in person or in writing. The decision of the Executive Committee shall be final.

Upon a final decision of the Amateur Status and Conduct Committee or the Executive Committee that a player has violated the Definition of an Amateur Golfer, such Committee may require the player to refrain or desist from specified actions as a condition of retaining his amateur status or declare the amateur status of the player forfeited. Such Committee shall notify the player, if possible, and may notify any interested golf association of any action taken under this paragraph.

3. Reinstatement

a. AUTHORITY AND PRINCIPLES

Either the Executive Committee or its Amateur Status and Conduct Committee may reinstate a player to amateur status and prescribe the probationary period necessary for reinstatement or deny reinstatement. In addition, the Amateur Status and Conduct Committee may authorize the staff of the USGA to reinstate a player to amateur status in routine situations where the violations do not warrant a reduction or increase in the normal two-year probationary period specified in Rule 2-3a(ii).

Each application for reinstatement shall be decided on its merits with consideration normally being given to the following principles:

(i) PROBATION

The professional holds an advantage over the amateur by reason of having devoted himself to the game as his profession; other persons violating the Rules of Amateur Status also obtain advantages not available to the amateur. They do not necessarily lose such advantage merely by deciding to cease violating the Rules.

Therefore, an applicant for reinstatement to amateur status shall undergo probation as prescribed.

Probation shall start from the date of the player's last violation of the Definition of an Amateur Golfer unless it is decided that it shall start from the date of the player's last known violation.

(ii) PROBATIONARY PERIOD

A probationary period of two years normally will be required. However, that period may be *extended or shortened.* Longer periods normally will be required when applicants have played extensively for prize money or have been previously reinstated; shorter periods often will be permitted when applicants have been in violation of the Rules one year or less. A probationary period of one year normally will be required when an applicant's only violation was to accept a prize of retail value exceeding $350 but less than $10,000.

(iii) PLAYERS OF NATIONAL PROMINENCE

Players of national prominence who have been in violation for more than five years normally will not be eligible for reinstatement.

(iv) STATUS DURING PROBATION

During probation an applicant for reinstatement shall conform with the Definition of an Amateur Golfer.

He shall not be eligible to enter competitions limited to amateurs except that he may enter competitions solely among members of a club of which he is a member, subject to the approval of the club. He may also, without prejudicing his application, enter, as an applicant for reinstatement, competitions which are not limited to amateurs but shall not accept any prize reserved for an amateur.

b. FORM OF APPLICATION

Each application for reinstatement shall be prepared, in duplicate, on forms provided by the USGA.

The application must be filed through a recognized amateur golf association in whose district the applicant resides. The association's recommendation, if any, will be considered. If the applicant is unknown to the association, this should be noted and the application forwarded to the USGA, without prejudice.

c. OBJECTION BY APPLICANT

If dissatisfied with the decision with respect to his application for reinstatement, the applicant may, by written notice to the staff within 30 days after being notified of the decision, appeal to the Executive Committee, in which case he shall be given reasonable notice of the next meeting of the Executive Committee at which the matter may be heard and shall be entitled to present his case in person or in writing. The decision of the Executive Committee shall be final.

USGA Policy on Gambling

The Definition of an Amateur Golfer provides that an amateur golfer is one who plays the game as a non-remunerative or non-profit-making sport. When gambling motives are introduced, problems can arise which threaten the integrity of the game.

The USGA does not object to participation in wagering among individual golfers or teams of golfers when participation in the wagering is limited to the players, the players may only wager on themselves or their teams, the sole source of all money won by players is advanced by the players and the primary purpose is the playing of the game for enjoyment.

The distinction between playing for prize money and gambling is essential to the validity of the Rules of Amateur Status. The following constitute golf wagering and not playing for prize money:

1. Participation in wagering among individual golfers.
2. Participation in wagering among teams.

Organized amateur events open to the general golfing public and designed and promoted to create cash prizes are not approved by the USGA. Golfers participating in such events without irrevocably waiving their right to cash prizes are deemed by the USGA to be playing for prize money.

The USGA is opposed to and urges its Member Clubs, all golf associations and all other sponsors of golf competitions to prohibit types of gambling such as: (1) Calcuttas, (2) other auction pools, (3) pari-mutuels and (4) any other forms of gambling organized for general participation or permitting participants to bet on someone other than themselves or their teams.

The Association may deny amateur status, entry in USGA Championships and membership on USGA teams for international competitions to players whose activities in connection with golf gambling, whether organized or individual, are considered by the USGA to be contrary to the best interests of golf.

PRINCIPAL CHANGES SINCE 1983

4-1. Form and Make of Clubs

Previously, flat sides were allowed on all grips. In the new Rules, the grips for all clubs, except putters, are required to be generally circular in cross-section. Flat sides will continue to be allowed in putter grips.

6-3. Time of Starting

The penalty of disqualification for late starting has been retained. However, a Note has been added to provide that a Committee may, in the conditions of a competition, modify the penalty for being up to five minutes late to loss of the first hole to be played in match play or two strokes in stroke play.

7. Practice

Amended to limit practice between holes to putts or chips on or near the putting green of the hole last played, any practice putting green or the next teeing ground. Such practice strokes must not be played from a hazard.

The prohibition against practice on a competition course before a stroke play round has been expanded to prohibit also the testing of the surface of any putting green on the course before such a round.

8-1. Advice

A note has been added permitting the Committee in charge of a team competition to allow each team to receive advice from one person such as a team captain or coach. However, this will not be permissible if an individual competition is being held concurrently with the team competition.

10. Order of Play

In all forms of match play, a player may require his opponent to replay a stroke played out of turn. Previously, in the case of three-ball and four-ball matches, a player could not require an opponent to replay a stroke played out of turn from through the green or in a hazard.

There is no penalty in stroke play for playing out of turn from the teeing ground or elsewhere unless competitors have agreed to play out of turn for the purpose of giving one of them an advantage. Previously, there was a penalty for deliberately playing out of turn from the teeing ground.

12-1. Searching for Ball

There is no penalty if a ball lying in casual water, ground under repair or a burrowing animal hole is accidentally moved during search. Previously, the player was exempt from penalty only if his ball was moved in probing for it.

18. Ball at Rest Moved

In all forms of play, if a player's ball at rest is moved by another ball, the moved ball must be replaced and the other ball played as it lies. There is no penalty except that in stroke play, if both balls lay on the putting green prior to the stroke, the player of the stroke would continue to be subject to a penalty of two strokes. Previously, in singles match play, if a player's ball at rest was moved by his opponent's ball, the player had the option of playing his ball as it lay or replacing it.

20-1. Lifting

Before lifting a ball anywhere on the course which must be replaced, its position must be marked. Previously, the Rules required marking the position of a ball before it was lifted on the putting green, but not elsewhere.

20-2a. Dropping

In dropping a ball under a Rule, the player is required to stand erect, hold the ball at shoulder height and arm's length and drop it. There is no restriction on the direction the player faces. If the dropped ball touches the player before or after it strikes the ground, the ball must be re-dropped. If the ball strikes the player's equipment, there is no penalty and the ball must be re-dropped.

20-3b. Lie of Ball to Be Placed or Replaced Altered.

Previously, if the lie of a ball to be placed or replaced was altered, the ball had to be placed in the nearest lie within *two* club-lengths which was most similar to that which it originally occupied. Two club-lengths have been reduced to *one* club-length and, in a bunker, the original lie has to be recreated and the ball placed in that lie.

22. Ball Interfering with or Assisting Play

In all forms of play, an opponent or fellow-competitor is permitted to lift his ball if he considers that it might assist any other player or have any other ball lifted if he considers that it might interfere with his play or assist the play of any other player. Formerly, in singles match play, if an opponent's ball was near the hole and the player considered it might be of assistance to him, the player could require his opponent to leave his ball there.

24-2. Immovable Obstructions

If a ball lies in a water hazard, the player is no longer entitled to relief if his swing or stance is interfered with by an immovable obstruction. On the other hand, if an immovable obstruction on a putting green, such as a sprinkler head, intervenes between a ball on the putting green and the hole, relief is permitted.

Exceptions have been added to the Rules giving relief from immovable obstructions, casual water, ground under repair and burrowing animal holes to withhold relief if (a) it is clearly unreasonable for the player to play a stroke because of interference by any other condition or (b) interference would occur only through use of an unnecessarily abnormal stance, swing or direction of play.

25-1. Casual Water, Ground Under Repair and Certain Damage to Course

If a ball lies in a water hazard, the player is no longer entitled to relief from a hole made by a burrowing animal, reptile or bird which interferes with his swing or stance.

30 and 31. Four-Ball Competition

In four-ball match play and stroke play one partner may represent the side for all or any part of a match or round. Thus, if a player does not arrive on time, his partner may play alone until the player arrives. The player may join his partner between the play of any two holes, but not during the play of a hole.